The Process-Focused Organization

A Transition Strategy for Success

Also available from ASQ Quality Press:

The Change Agent's Guide to Radical Improvement
Ken Miller

The Recipe for Simple Business Improvement
David W. Till

*Making Change Work: Practical Tools for Overcoming
Human Resistance to Change*
Brien Palmer

Transformational Leadership: Creating Organizations of Meaning
Stephen Hacker and Tammy Roberts

Business Process Improvement Toolbox
Bjørn Andersen

To request a complimentary catalog of ASQ Quality Press publications,
call 800-248-1946, or visit our Web site at http://qualitypress.asq.org.

The Process-Focused Organization

A Transition Strategy for Success

Robert Gardner

ASQ Quality Press
Milwaukee, Wisconsin

American Society for Quality, Quality Press, Milwaukee 53203
© 2004 by ASQ
All rights reserved. Published 2004
Printed in the United States of America

12 11 10 09 08 07 06 05 04   5 4 3 2 1

Library of Congress Cataloging-in-Publication Data

Gardner, Robert, 1947–.
  The process-focused organization : a transition strategy for success /
Robert Gardner.
    p. cm.
  Includes bibliographical references and index.
  ISBN 0-87389-627-0 (soft cover, perfect bound : alk. paper)
  1. Reengineering (Management) 2. Process control. 3. Organizational
change. 4. Organizational effectiveness. 5. Industrial management. I. Title.

HD58.87.G37 2004
658.4'063—dc22   2004006797

Publisher: William A. Tony
Acquisitions Editor: Annemieke Hytinen
Project Editor: Paul O'Mara
Production Administrator: Randall Benson
Special Marketing Representative: Matt Meinholz

ASQ Mission: The American Society for Quality advances individual,
organizational, and community excellence worldwide through learning,
quality improvement, and knowledge exchange.

Attention Bookstores, Wholesalers, Schools, and Corporations: ASQ Quality
Press books, videotapes, audiotapes, and software are available at quantity
discounts with bulk purchases for business, educational, or instructional use.
For information, please contact ASQ Quality Press at 800-248-1946, or write to
ASQ Quality Press, P.O. Box 3005, Milwaukee, WI 53201-3005.

To place orders or to request a free copy of the ASQ Quality Press Publications
Catalog, including ASQ membership information, call 800-248-1946. Visit our
Web site at www.asq.org or http://qualitypress.asq.org.

 Printed on acid-free paper

Quality Press
600 N. Plankinton Avenue
Milwaukee, Wisconsin 53203
Call toll free 800-248-1946
Fax 414-272-1734
www.asq.org
http://qualitypress.asq.org
http://standardsgroup.asq.org
E-mail: authors@asq.org

AMERICAN SOCIETY
FOR QUALITY™

Table of Contents

Preface

The concept of *process* continues to gain momentum in the business community. Although process has been around for some time, the most recent wave (under the Six Sigma banner) has fueled a resurgence of interest that is causing more organizations to seek ways to make process work for them. To be sure, many of us have seen examples of companies that have learned how to exploit the power of process to enable remarkable improvements in performance and to establish clear competitive advantage. We have probably seen many more organizations, however, launch process initiatives that deliver mixed or even disappointing results. These mixed results may explain, in part at least, why the average life expectancy of contemporary process programs runs around two to three years.[1]

The process movement has been on the scene for many years, with several reincarnations that have promised profound and lasting results. Although the movement has developed influential supporters and captured tremendous attention at times, I believe it has not provided sufficiently complete answers to the central questions regarding enterprise performance:

- How can we become more responsive to the marketplace?

- How can we improve the value of our products and services?

- How can we improve the efficiency of our operations?

- How can we improve the connection between leadership intentions and organizational capabilities?

- How can we more effectively utilize the potential of our people?

Although the process movement may not have provided sufficient answers to these questions, I remain convinced that process lies at the center of the answer.

Contemporary process programs work within the architecture of the traditional organization. It can be difficult for these programs to solve the relevant problems we face when the root causes of the problems frequently stem from the nature of the traditional organizational design. Traditional organizations do some things well, and some things not so well. Managing cross-functional business processes is not one of the things traditional organizations do very well. Contemporary process programs also tend to place disproportionate emphasis on process improvement at the expense of process management. Process management, which is integral to sustaining performance, involves more than process control plans: it involves managing the relationships between enterprise goals, strategy, and business processes; managing the alignment between enterprise structures, systems, and processes; and managing enterprise performance via key business processes.

There is an alternative organizational form that seeks to attend to these needs. This organizational form, which is commonly referred to as a *process-focused organization,* recognizes the integrative and aligning nature of process. Process-focused organizations are different from traditional organizations in several key ways: (1) they design and manage end-to-end business processes rather than tasks, (2) they measure and manage process-level results instead of departmental efficiency, and (3) they think in terms of customer goals instead of localized functional goals.[2] The process-focused organization offers a more powerful and complete paradigm for exploiting the power of process.

Although there is considerable information available that describes the virtues of process focus, there is little that describes a road map for attaining the characteristics of the process-focused organization. This book seeks to fill that gap by offering such a road map.

The road map presented in this book is designed to guide the transition from a functionally managed organization to a process-focused organization. It guides the establishment of the operating structures necessary to manage and continuously improve key cross-functional business processes, while ensuring continued alignment between those processes and key business drivers, strategies, and goals. It utilizes process improvement and process management as key enablers, but not as the overarching management framework. The approach described in this book is built around three principle components: (1) an operating model that describes the key operating structures and relationships, (2) a process improvement road map to guide process work, and (3) a transformation strategy that guides the journey to process focus. The operating model defines the structures and responsibilities needed to form our foundations, the process improvement road map describes a simple five-step approach to systematically improving the capability of business processes, and the transformation strategy combines the model and road map into a straightforward plan for navigating the journey to process focus.

The concepts and approaches shared in this book were influenced by the many people I've worked with or studied over the years. The operating systems model evolved from the ideas taught by Dr. Michael Hammer, while the road map was inspired by the Software Engineering Institute's capability maturity model. Both ideas were refined as I applied them in various business settings (ranging from manufacturing to commercial software and public utilities). The transformation strategy, however, was the product of a specific engagement involving a large, traditionally managed utility organization that was seeking to transform itself to a process-focused organization. The strategy was the product of months of collaborative effort involving many people. This is where we tested and reshaped the ideas presented in this book. Although I have moved on, the transformation continues to unfold at this organization.

Since these components (operating model, improvement road map, and transformation strategy) will always be a work in progress, I've hesitated to describe them formally and share them publicly. At the urging of several colleagues, however, I realized that it was time to share these ideas with others who are navigating the journey to process focus. You're now holding the result.

It's important to point out that this book describes a pathway to a vision. The vision is clear and certain, however, the pathway presented here is not the only way to attain the vision. There are, I am sure, alternative approaches that may be followed. Although the approach described here is not positioned as the only way, it is a highly integrated approach that should not be modified without considerable thought.

Acknowledgments

Although the years have blurred many of the names, there are numerous people who have powerfully influenced my development and, therefore, the ideas reflected in this book. Key among these are W. Edwards Deming, Michael Hammer, Peter Keen, Geary Rumler, Allan Brache, Eliyahu Goldratt, James Womack, Daniel Jones, Peter Senge, and Steven Covey. On a more personal level, I would like to acknowledge Horton Russell for giving me the initial opportunity to work in this highly challenging area, Michael Tatham for helping me see the common sense to process work, Mark Nelson for the many hours of debate and collaboration while working out the elements of the transformation strategy, and Melanie Harris for painstakingly proofreading the material you're holding. I thank each of these people for sharing their insights.

Part I

Perspectives On Performance

1

The Performance Challenge

A BRIEF HISTORY OF TIME

Business enterprises are constantly challenged to improve performance. The plain fact is that when operating in competitive environments, we must continuously learn how to do things better, faster, and cheaper or we will end up operating at a significant disadvantage. It's as simple as the mantra of a past instructor, "if you aren't getting better, you're getting worse." This inexorable reality causes us to always be on the lookout for the latest improvement technique in the hope it will help us meet these challenges.

When I became involved in quality and performance improvement in the middle '80s, total quality management (TQM) was all the rage. There was an abundance of pundits and practitioners telling us how TQM would change the fortunes of our businesses. TQM was a natural response to a real problem. It taught that quality is a significant differentiator in the marketplace and that it costs us less to prevent quality problems than to detect and correct them. ISO 9000 rose as the standard for enabling organizations to integrate quality practices into their operations.

A few years later we saw the beginnings of the Malcolm Baldrige National Quality Award program. Baldrige extended and clarified many of the key lessons of TQM by incorporating them into an integrated systems model of the high-performing organization. Although the model and supporting criteria replaced the ambiguity of TQM with clear structures and checklists, its complexity was daunting to many of us. Moreover, what the model gave us in terms of a highly complete and integrated package, it lacked in its ability to deliver quick results. These issues seemed to relegate Baldrige to the shadows for most of its life. That's truly unfortunate because Baldrige teaches us valuable lessons about the interdependent nature of the systems and processes that comprise our organizations and determine their outcomes.

In the early '90s, reengineering took us by storm. Whereas the previous movements emphasized product quality and incremental improvement, reengineering talked about process and quantum improvement. This was an exciting time for those of us who sought to implement bold changes to our organizations in pursuit of big-bang improvements. Although reengineering did teach us about the relevance of process, it failed to provide methods that would consistently deliver expected results. Ultimately, reengineering became associated with downsizing and fell off the charts almost as fast as it arrived. It seemed that we needed simpler and less demanding approaches, and reengineering was neither.

Following on the heels of reengineering was the early process improvement movement. While this movement retained the emphasis on process, it reframed reengineering in more practical terms—by replacing quantum with incremental. Although this work used the same tools we'd learned with TQM, it added clear methodologies to focus and guide our efforts.

Now we find ourselves in the midst of the Six Sigma wave. Six Sigma has attracted tremendous attention, with more and more organizations jumping on the bandwagon. The wave is fueled by the claims of practitioners that unparalleled performance gains can be obtained by simply fixing process problems.

As I consider the history and future of the performance improvement field, however, I become less certain than many of my colleagues that the current movement will deliver the profound and lasting results being promised. As I look back, it occurs to me that each of the previous waves began with great expectations that were never quite fully realized. Although TQM certainly enabled meaningful improvements along the way, it was plagued by its philosophical nature, lack of clear approaches, and long maturation time. Reengineering suffered a similar demise as organizations learned that big-bang improvements were incredibly difficult and risky undertakings. ISO 9000 continues to consume considerable resources in documenting and auditing quality systems that, from my experience, frequently allow the ongoing production of poor quality. And, frankly, I support Dr. Michael Beer's observation that there is little reason to believe that Six Sigma will be any more successful that the programs of earlier years.[1]

Sometimes practitioners dismiss these shortcomings as implementation deficiencies. I believe there is much more to it than that. Early in my process training I was taught to blame the process, not the people. It seems that those of us who craft process programs should apply this lesson to our own work as well.

The Process Paradox
(aka Success without Achievement)

It's important to note that as these waves were being implemented, we consistently saw claims of significant gains in performance. The current wave, in particular, lays claim to extraordinary results. What concerns me is that, in spite of these claims, the overall performance of our organizations doesn't seem to have really improved that much. Peter Keen supports this observation in *The Process Edge* when he describes examples of organizations implementing successful improvement programs while, at the same time, overall performance fails to improve, or even slips.[2] This phenomenon, which Keen calls the *process paradox,* occurs when organizations fail to focus on enhancing their core value-creating processes. From my experience, another contributor to the paradox involves the way organizations measure and report improvement results. The key observation is that, regardless of the reason, it is clearly possible to have success without achievement.

Business enterprises adopt process improvement programs for one reason—results! For that reason, business managers commonly seek an immediate return from their investment, while practitioners sell their services based on fulfilling those expectations. Complying with the demand for quick returns may help sell programs, but it does little to reshape the thinking and practices required to sustain improvement programs and their results over the long term. If you think about it, picking the proverbial "low-hanging fruit" simply reinforces old paradigms, instead of asking us to challenge them. While this approach may give the illusion of quick improvement, it can be another contributor to Keen's process paradox.

Process improvement work involves a fundamental trade-off—where investments are made today in return for future benefits. Failure to acknowledge this trade-off tends to promote several dysfunctional patterns:

• *Short-circuiting the essentials.* Successful performance improvement programs are built on solid foundations. Skipping essential steps, or working steps out of order, only impedes program effectiveness over the long term. Too often, we see well-conceived implementation plans short-circuited by senior managers who are unwilling to perform essential steps. When this occurs, the seeds of failure are sown, and the chances of program success are greatly diminished.

• *Bogus improvements.* When improvement practitioners are placed under enormous pressure to produce immediate and substantial results, there's a tendency to manipulate and exaggerate outcomes. When this occurs, programs may become superficial, promoting a form-over-substance climate. Once the basic integrity of a program is suspect, credibility and motivation falter, and the program begins to die. This isn't just cynical speculation; I've personally seen it happen more times that I'd like to admit.

• *Premature harvesting.* When we are anxious to take improvements to the bottom line, we sometimes seek to harvest gains too early. Gains take time to materialize (to offset investments and to assimilate learning curves) and need to be reinvested in the program. Of course, bogus improvements can never really be harvested.

Studies by Hendricks and Singhal have shown that the long-run stock performance of firms who receive quality awards is far higher (38 percent to 46 percent) than companies who did not receive awards.[3] These stock performance improvements only occurred after five years of implementation, however, making it highly unlikely that they were recognized as being a consequence of the quality programs. It is also unlikely that the quality programs that drove these improvements were still in existence when the results finally did manifest themselves. The fact that real results have a long incubation time indicates that improvement must be approached as a long-term process.

While it is clear that results sell programs, I remain convinced that an absolute focus on immediate results fuels the patterns just outlined in ways that ultimately defeat our improvement programs. When these dysfunctions occur, our organizations are placed under even greater pressure than before. This pressure will tend to fuel another round of counterproductive behaviors that ultimately destroys the self-reinforcing dynamic we are seeking. While I believe practitioners must move quickly when conducting improvement work, management must understand that improvement takes time to hit the bottom line.

Although practitioners must move quickly, they must avoid acting too hastily. Once, when discussing the results of a process improvement effort with a long-term manager, I learned that the very same process problem had been fixed previously, at least twice. Is it possible that the previous fixes had not stuck because of incomplete deployments or inadequate follow-up? If moving too fast produces incomplete solutions, then fast can actually be the slow and costly approach.

Even when the dysfunctions just outlined are not operating, results may not always be what they seem. A while back I observed a situation in which an enterprise had previously implemented a process change that professed a multimillion dollar cost savings. The enterprise had worked hard to implement the change and was proud of the hard dollar savings it produced. To this day, executive management touts the change as an industry best practice. Upon closer examination, however, one would find that the localized improvement had significant adverse impacts across the enterprise and its value stream. This examination would reveal that 29 percent of the savings was offset by increased operating costs in another department, 13 percent was offset by decreased revenues directly attributable to the change, 36 percent was pushed to the customer as increased cost of doing business, and 44 percent was lost as material waste that had to be picked up by the market-place as increased product cost. When we add the numbers up, 122 percent of the savings was offset by some adverse outcome. Although this work was based on honest effort to drive results to the bottom line, it lost sight of the need to tend to the value proposition of the enterprise. If we define achievement as improving the ability of the system to deliver improved value at reduced cost, then this is a clear example of success without achievement.

Level-Setting Process Improvement

As we look toward the future, I believe we must build on the lessons of the past and continue to advance our understanding and mastery of the factors that determine organizational performance. The journey hasn't ended with process improvement—process improvement is just a step along the way. What this means in the near term is that while process improvement can be a powerful tool, it isn't the complete solution to performance improvement. We may want to consider the following cautions when engaging in process improvement work:

• *Process improvement is not a magic bullet.* Many of us who adopt process improvement programs are led to believe that process improvement will single-handedly produce profound and lasting improvements that will fundamentally change the fortunes of our enterprises. I, for one, am doubt-ful that current process improvement practices have the power to funda-mentally change the fortunes of the enterprises that practice it. To be more specific, I believe that simply applying reductionalistic process problem-solving techniques to solve process problems while ignoring the broader issues of how we design and manage our organizational structures and sys-tems is incomplete thinking. Actually, it seems to me that these broader issues are frequently the real root causes to many of the performance prob-lems facing us today. That's not to say process improvement is a bad thing, because it isn't. But it does have clear limits that must be understood and respected. The gap between expectations and capability to meet those expectations may eventually fuel discontent with yet another wave.

• *Process improvement has limited application.* The popularity of process improvement can result in it being applied to situations where it is ineffective or even powerless. Abraham Maslow's maxim, "He that is good with a hammer thinks everything is a nail," applies to process improvement as well. It's not uncommon to see an organization acquire a methodology and then try to apply it to every problem in sight. Process improvement, like Maslow's hammer, is a tool that should be carefully selected and configured based on the type of problem being addressed. Applying process improvement to nonprocess problems (such as poor business plans, ineffective organizational designs, organizational misalignment, or insufficient competencies) may be a waste of time.

• *Process improvement isn't the final answer.* Although I'm a passionate believer in the relevance of process, I'm convinced we have further work ahead of us before we can understand how to fully exploit the power of process. *To fully exploit the power of process, we must learn how to link process to organizational strategy, how to integrate process with organizational structures and systems, and how to proactively manage processes—not just fix them.*

I concur with the caution offered by Geary Rummler and Alan Bache about the danger of thinking we have the final answer to performance improvement when they remind us that "managing to meet the challenge of change is a complex and complicated task. Piecemeal approaches that are assumed to be the answer are as dangerous as no response at all. These efforts can absorb vast resources as they lull an organization into thinking it is addressing its needs."[4] I, too, am concerned that as long as we believe we have the answer in our grasp, we will be less inclined to continue the search for greater understanding of organizational performance. I remain convinced that we don't quite yet have the answer and that we still have more to learn before we declare victory. Although the lessons of the process movement are an integral part of the learning curve, they are, as Steven Covey might remind us "necessary, but insufficient."[5]

FACING THE FUTURE

The Business of Business

Creating value for customers is the foundation for every successful business system.[6] Value, more than any other single factor, has been shown to be the best predictor of customer loyalty and the best leading indicator of market share and competitiveness.[7] This implies that the key to achieving sustainable improvements in performance is by building sustainable improvements in value delivered.

Although value is commonly described as quality over cost, a more useful and complete description is offered by Robert Woodruff and Sarah Gardial in *Know Your Customer.*[8] Value, according to Woodruff and Gardial, is a perception that is shaped by the consequences of using a product or service. To the degree that these consequences are aligned with a customer's goals and needs, a product or service possesses value (see Figure 1.1). A key implication of this model is that the degree of value present is as closely related to the customer's intended use of the product or service as it is to the attributes of the product or service.[9] In other words, we cannot begin to understand or measure value without first understanding customer-perceived goals and needs.

Although we frequently see measurements of customer satisfaction, we rarely see measurements of customer value delivered. This is unfortunate, because value is a more powerful and useful performance indicator. This is because, to a large extent, customer satisfaction is simply an emotional response to the degree of perceived value received. Therefore, when we measure satisfaction, we are measuring customer responses relative to perceptions of value previously received. Customer dissatisfaction has to occur before we are able to sense it. When we measure value, however, we are measuring future satisfaction. This puts us in the position to proactively manage satisfaction before it occurs.

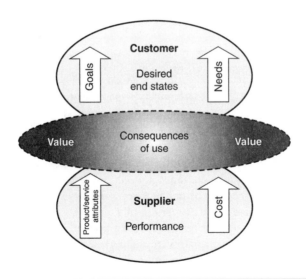

Figure 1.1   Customer value model.

Performance Challenges

In seeking to create and deliver value to our customers and stakeholders, we face a broad spectrum of performance challenges. To be successful over the long run, it stands to reason that our approaches to performance improvement must carefully address these challenges. A few of these challenges and the potential role of process in addressing them include:

1. *Execution speed.* Organizations must execute faster than before. The organization with the shortest product design to deployment cycle time will be much more responsive to the shifting needs of the marketplace, while the organization with the shortest order fulfillment cycle time will be more responsive to meeting near-term customer needs. Today, we find that many organizations have exceedingly long lead times along their value chain. Most of this time is filled with idle time, where designs, products, and orders sit around waiting for approvals or resources. A major contributor to slowness are the handoffs that occur between the various organizational units that participate in our processes. These handoffs are the source of delays and non-value-adding work.

Process work can help us improve execution speed by giving us visibility to the use of time as products and services flow through our organizations. Lean techniques, in particular, have demonstrated tremendous power in identifying and removing constraints to flow. This work, however, faces a formidable adversary in the form of the functional structures that promote local efficiency at the expense of flow and speed.

2. *Waste.* Organizations encounter considerable waste in the production of products and services. From my experience, it's not uncommon to see non-value-adding work account for 80 percent of the effort expended in the production of products and services. Much of this effort is consumed in checking, rechecking, correcting the results of previous work, or supervising or coordinating the efforts of others. As mentioned previously, organizations also waste large amounts of time. We frequently see process lead times of days or weeks while only a few minutes of work effort is applied during that time. Long cycle times not only make us slow and unresponsive, they add to the cost of our products and services in several ways. First, as products and service orders sit idly, they continue to collect costs. Second, the longer the process queue, the greater the need to build up costly work-in-process inventory to support service-level requirements. And third, the longer products are in work-in-process status, the greater the risk of obsolescence.

The traditional functional organization contributes to these types of waste by imposing handoffs along the value-creating processes, by isolating decision points along the flow of value, and by adding the layers of management overhead required to coordinate the various units comprising the value stream. Moreover, the functional organization's emphasis on local efficiency tends to promote waste in the form of overproduction.[10]

It should be clear that process work can help us see the various forms of waste that exist in our processes. What may not be as clear is the perspective that is required to be able to effectively see waste. Waste elimination is not something that can be performed at the subprocess level; it must be performed from the perspective of the full end-to-end process. This means that we must evaluate the value of all actions in terms of the total process, not in terms of local considerations.

3. *Quality.* At more than any other time in our history, quality is a requirement of doing business. Although we've made great strides in delivered quality, most organizations are generally limited to monitoring the quality of outcomes and implementing corrections only when those outcomes become unfavorable. Since the work of detecting and correcting errors is clearly non-value-adding expense, however, we are challenged with finding ways to eliminate the need for this type of work by developing processes that are capable of getting it right the first time.

Process work provides the opportunity and tools required to proactively manage the quality of outcomes by managing the upstream determinants of those outcomes. Many organizations successfully utilize quality function deployment (QFD) to discover customer quality requirements and to translate them into their process designs, design of experiments (DOE) to statistically understand and validate process design performance, and statistical process control (SPC) to monitor and manage process behavior on an ongoing basis.

4. *Alignment.* Organizational effectiveness is determined, in part, by the degree of alignment between the various components comprising the organization. Today, it is not uncommon to see organizational components operating in ways that are detrimental to the performance of other components. For example, when purchasing departments strive to drive down raw material costs in the name of efficiency, it is very possible to see manufacturing costs increase correspondingly due to quality or conversion issues. And many of us have grown accustomed to the problems that occur downstream when our sales organizations overpromise to customers in the name of getting the order. Poor organizational alignment can significantly degrade the performance of the enterprise as a whole.

From my experience, misalignment is less a result of maverick behavior than it is a result of how the organizational components are measured and managed. Consider, for example, the way most organizations deploy performance objectives through a system of downward decomposition through the organizational silos. In this approach, the goals of higher-level components are decomposed and passed to subordinate components. While this assures that organizational objectives are aligned vertically, along the chain of command, it ignores the need for horizontal alignment, along the flow of value creation. As a result, it is not uncommon to see operating units fully satisfy their objectives while the cross-functional processes they support flounder or fail. Moreover, it is not uncommon to see one department implement process changes for the sake of that department, and even be praised for its efforts, only to find later that the changes degrade the performance of other departments.

We also need to do a better job of connecting reward and performance! Today, it is not uncommon to find that rewards are more closely linked to how well we look internally than to how well we look to the customers we serve. Instead, we should strive to develop stronger connections between individual reward and the performance of the processes we support.

Process can help with alignment, but it alone does not address the broader organizational structures and systems that establish the context within which processes operate. It stands to reason that fixing a process that is operating in a misaligned organization will probably fail to deliver expected results.

Addressing alignment requires that we learn how to manage the horizontal dimension of performance as the primary determinant of success. To do this we must: (1) establish clear enterprise performance goals, (2) deploy these goals to our value-creating business processes, (3) design our organizational structures and systems to support the value-creating processes, and (4) manage performance by managing process performance. Unfortunately, there is little in the repertoire of current improvement approaches that effectively addresses these needs.

5. *Manageability.* Businesses exist to produce value for stakeholders, yet management generally has little visibility to the processes that create value. In most organizations, management is left with trying to manage the functional components of its processes without having visibility to the quality of the relationships between these components. This leaves managers with only being able to manage their organizations vertically, not horizontally along the flow of value. As a consequence, managers sometimes find themselves blindsided by problems that occur without warning, even though all performance indicators are operating nominally. Even worse, since the root causes to these problems are not visible, our efforts to resolve them frequently miss the mark as well.

Although cost management is a primary concern of enterprise managers, we find that traditional accounting systems provide little insight regarding the true cost of producing our goods and services. While we know precisely what our departments cost, we only have a rough idea of what our products and services cost. Pooled costing systems may subsidize unprofitable products and penalize profitable products, making it is difficult to know the real picture. Process work can help us meet this challenge by providing a framework for establishing costing approaches that yield more accurate pictures of our product costs. Many organizations utilize variations of activity-based costing (ABC) techniques to conduct diagnostic evaluations of their business processes. These diagnostics are especially powerful since they describe process performance using the language of business—dollars.

Managers are also challenged with doing a better job of proactively managing outcomes. Today, we see the widespread use of trailing indicators to gauge performance. Although trailing indicators may do a good job of telling us what has happened, they are of little value when it comes to proactively managing outcomes. Process provides us the means to statistically understand and manage performance. Later, we will introduce a process measurement and control model that is designed to help us proactively manage process outcomes.

6. *Adaptability.* Long-term business health is largely a function of how well organizations adapt to change. It's interesting to note that just 18 months after Peters and Waterman published their list of excellent companies, 33 percent had dropped from the list—in part because they had failed to adapt to changes in the external environment.[11]

Traditional organizations seek to manage the future by planning for it. This is not always an effective strategy, however, since the future is largely unknowable. There is significant evidence that suggests that organizations that are able to adapt to the future, regardless of the shape it takes, are more effective at dealing with the future than those who plan for it.

The ability to adapt is closely linked to the ability to learn and change. Learning must be continuous and rely on feedback systems that are timely and sensitive to the right things. Change (ability) requires that operating methods be designed to operate somewhat dynamically, instead of being absolutely rigid and fixed. Both of these requirements represent significant challenges for the traditional organization.

An adaptive enterprise can also make high-quality decisions quickly. This means that we must have the right information readily available to the right people at the right time. This generally involves designing jobs to enable and empower frontline people to make decisions in real time, while the moment of truth is still at hand. Unfortunately, the traditional functional organization tends to draw authority away from frontline personnel in the name of control. It seems that some of the lessons of scientific management need to be reversed so we can replace the time-consuming, resource-wasting approval practices with more adaptive approaches. Linking jobs to process performance, instead of functional efficiencies, can help in addressing this challenge.

Summary

I suspect that most would agree that these challenges are real and that they describe some of the key differentiators to sustained enterprise success. Therefore, it is reasonable to expect that our approaches to performance improvement must consider these broader, system-level issues if our efforts are to be successful over the long term. Although the science of reductionalism has benefited us in many ways, it seems that we need to adopt a broader systems perspective to performance improvement to make our gains real and sustainable.

Rummler and Brache share their perspective regarding the performance challenge in their classic book *Improving Performance: How to Manage the White Space in the Organization Chart* when they say:

> Whether the concern is quality, customer focus, productivity, cycle time, or cost, the underlying issue is performance. In our opinion, most managers have not been able to respond effectively to these challenges because they have failed to create an infrastructure for systematic and continuous improvement of performance. We believe that their shortcoming does not lie in the understanding of the problem—rather the majority of managers simply do not understand the variables that influence organization and individual performance.[12]

2

Evolving the Process Paradigm

THE CURRENT PROCESS PARADIGM

While the concept of process is certainly central to performance improvement, the paradigm that drives many of our current process improvement programs seems to be incomplete. The following observations are offered as a generalized view of how process improvement programs tend to operate. To the degree that any of these observations reflect reality, the underlying paradigm is not grasping the full potential of process:

• As currently practiced, process improvement programs tend to view processes as cost pools from which near-term economic gain can be extracted, not as key enterprise assets that must be managed and improved on a continuing basis. This phenomenon seems to be fueled by both the push for quick results and an insufficient understanding of the relevance of process to long-term organizational capability.

• Process improvement programs tend to embrace time frames and tool sets that result in narrowly defined problem spaces, thereby yielding a series of localized improvements, which may or may not improve the performance of the overall system. Goldratt taught us valuable lessons about the potential for localized improvements to negatively impact system performance in *The Goal.*[1]

• Although process improvement programs make extensive use of measurement to conduct analysis and report improvement results, these measurements are generally reported at the local level, not at the system level. Since local improvements do not necessarily translate to system-level gains, it is possible for system performance to actually be declining at the same time practitioners are reporting significant improvements.[2]

• Process improvement programs do not provide a framework for systematically advancing the capability and manageability of processes. If processes are, in fact, key enterprise assets, then our programs must direct us toward actions that improve the effectiveness, efficiency, and manageability of our processes. There is an order to process work, and working improvement steps out of order can waste valuable time and energy. For example, it is of little practical value to seek process capability for a process that has not attained repeatability, nor is it reasonable to expect repeatability when a process has not been standardized. Generally, there is little in contemporary programs that moves our processes along a continuum of improvement.

• Process improvement programs tend to ignore the broader organizational system, which results in practitioners ignoring the very factors that cause many performance problems in the first place. These factors, which include how we plan, structure, and manage our organizations, are powerful determinants of our ability to impact and sustain enterprise performance. The failure to explicitly deal with issues of organizational alignment is a common shortcoming of contemporary process work.

• Process improvement programs do not sufficiently engage organizational leadership. Apart from showing support and paying for resources, most programs ask leaders for very little. The beliefs and actions of leaders send powerful signals throughout the organization, and if these signals continue unchanged, the chances of change are greatly diminished. Leadership is needed to break old patterns as well as to inspire new ones. If leaders continue pulling the same levers as before, the organization will respond by perpetuating the patterns of old. This means that our improvement programs must provide new levers for leaders to pull so they are viably connected to and reinforcing new organizational patterns.

The contemporary process improvement paradigm must be expanded if we are to increase the power of process work. A more complete paradigm would take a significantly different view of processes. It would understand that processes are what produce the value that is delivered to the marketplace. It would acknowledge that processes bring to life the competencies of the enterprise, that processes are the glue that hold the organizational components together, and that processes are what translate strategy into action. Moreover, it would understand that what really needs to be managed are the organization's processes, not its functions.

Some of the tactical challenges that must be resolved by this paradigm include: (1) how to establish clear linkages between enterprise strategy and our value-creating business processes, (2) how to better understand and manage system-level performance, (3) how to manage hierarchical organizations and cross-functional processes simultaneously, and (4) how to align supporting structures and systems to enable effective process operations. Although these are considerable challenges, the failure to successfully meet them will limit the ability of programs to produce meaningful and lasting results. Unfortunately, they are rarely addressed by existing programs or methodologies.

THE CONTEMPORARY ORGANIZATION

Most contemporary organizations are designed based on the functional hierarchy (see Figure 2.1). This organizational form is based on the

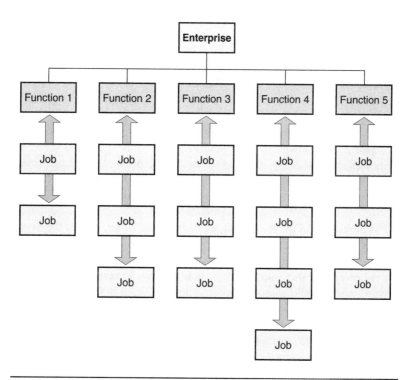

Figure 2.1 Functional organization—goals are deployed downward to jobs via functional hierarchy, while performance is assessed upwardly.

principles of control and specialization. To enable control, the chain of command is clear, with jobs reporting to the functional managers above them and enterprise goals being deployed downwardly through the functional silos. To enable specialization, jobs tend to be narrowly defined, with clear limits on authority and accountability. The primacy of the chain of command is reflected in all aspects of organizational life in the functional organization.

The functional organization is designed to operate in static environments, where control and stability are the primary determinants of success. It is not, however, a particularly adaptive or responsive design.

Since decisions are made by managers in the functional organization, information must flow upward before it can flow horizontally, which introduces potential delays and distortions in the flow of information. The strong division of responsibility that facilitates control and specialization in the functional organization also causes performance to be managed in isolation, resulting in localized efficiency as the primary measure of organizational effectiveness. In this environment, subordinate managers tend to perceive other functions as enemies, rather than partners. The resulting silo culture prevents interdepartmental issues from being resolved between peers at lower operating levels, which forces managers to divert their attention from strategic concerns to handle routine operational issues. Functional organizations also tend to evolve into tall structures to accommodate the levels of management required to coordinate the differentiated components.

Goal deployment in the functional organization is generally handled by cascading goals downward through the functional silos. Unfortunately, this approach has the effect of disconnecting local performance from system performance. Actually, vertically aligned goals that do not recognize the horizontal interdependences of processes can promote suboptimization across the value stream. As a consequence, it is possible to see high levels of local success in the functional organization at the same time the overall system is underachieving or failing. Consider, for example, the fact that individual or local performance reviews regularly outpace the performance of the enterprise they support. Although it stands to reason that enterprise performance should reasonably correlate with local performance, experience has shown that the two phenomena seem to operate in a disconnected fashion. Although vertically deployed goals do promote alignment, it seems that this alignment occurs in the wrong direction. Wouldn't it be more effective if our goals were aligned horizontally, in support of the enterprise value creation stream?

The Missing Ingredients

When we examine the organizational chart of a functional organization we may notice that three of the most important ingredients to enterprise success are strikingly absent. These include: (1) the customers served by the enterprise, (2) the products and services provided to the customers, and (3) the processes used to produce and deliver the products and services. These omissions contribute to the fact that functional organizations tend to construct business processes that are fragmented, inefficient, and unresponsive to customers (as illustrated via the dashed lines in Figure 2.2). Moreover, managing overall performance is difficult in the functional organizational because the cross-functional value-creating business processes are simply not visible.

Because the cross-functional value creating processes are largely invisible in the functional organization, process improvement efforts generally work at the component level. As a result, improvements are usually implemented via localized efforts that may or may not positively impact the performance of the total system or be sustained by the system over the long term. When this occurs, we may actually praise and reward the very efforts that

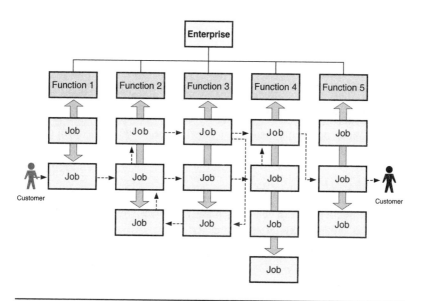

Figure 2.2 In a functional organization, processes meander through silos, imposing numerous handoffs, decision points, and rework.

degrade system-level performance! A key implication of this apparent paradox is that we must learn how to measure performance at the system level.

LESSONS FROM SYSTEMS THINKING

Systems theory taught us long ago that organizations are composed of differentiated and interdependent subsystems. Whereas the science of reductionalism focuses on the parts, systems thinking focuses on the whole—that is, the system. Systems thinking reminds us that before we can effectively understand and manage organizational performance, we must understand and mange the overall system of performance. While it may be interesting to describe an organization as a culture or as a set of power dynamics, at some point it must be described in terms of what it does and how it does it, that is, how it performs as a system.[3] Systems thinking also reminds us that our efforts to change system-level performance by working on component subsystems in isolation may not work, may not last, or may even suboptimize overall system performance.

When designing performance improvement programs, remember the following:

- Systems exist to meet system-level goals.

- Sustained system-level performance requires the continuous alignment of component subsystems toward the system goals.

- Changes to component subsystems fuel tension or perhaps even disorder in the total system.

- When one component of a system is optimized, the system often suboptimizes.

- Systems tend to counteract disruptions to component systems, regardless if they are beneficial or not.

- Effective system change generally involves simultaneous change to numerous system components.

It's essential to recognize that every system is built for a purpose and that every action by a component subsystem should be judged in terms of its impact on this purpose. This implies that before we can effectively deal with improvement to any system, we must first define the system's purpose and the measurements that will enable us to judge the impact of any local change on system goals.[4]

Although these points are not new, we seem to forget them when we design our performance improvement programs. We develop vision and strategy to set direction, we reorganize structures till the cows come home, we train to inspire and equip our people, we adjust performance management systems to promote desired behaviors, we listen to our customers and manage our suppliers, and last, but not least, we continuously improve our processes. Yet, in spite of these actions, I'm not convinced that we've fundamentally changed the capabilities of our organizations via our improvement programs. While it is clear that each of these actions has merit, the problem is that performing them in isolation ignores the need for integration and alignment. In other words, we're not connecting the dots.

I believe that *process* provides the key integrative element required to effectively link and align the components that comprise organizations. I believe process has the power to connect the dots if we expand the current process paradigm to include a broader systems perspective.

THE NATURAL LAWS OF PROCESS WORK

When talking about improving personal effectiveness, Steven Covey introduces us to the concept of natural laws.[5] Covey explains that these laws are there, determining outcomes, whether we acknowledge them or not. As an example, the law of the harvest tells us that the size of the harvest is related to the quality of soil preparation. My experience has shown that process work abides by natural laws as well. No matter how much we want a result, no matter how hard we urge others to get a result, or no matter how much we're willing to pay for a result—there are some things that simply are as they are. Our choice is to either ignore these laws and suffer the consequences, or acknowledge and assimilate them. Ether way, they're there, determining outcomes. When considering a process-based performance improvement initiative, the following natural laws are worth remembering[6]:

1. *Without an end in mind, you won't get there.* The absence of a clear purpose when launching an improvement program can be a fatal flaw. Without purpose there is no framework for establishing priorities, aligning efforts, or judging success. Therefore, it is essential to have a clear picture of what we're seeking to accomplish before launching an improvement program. This picture will ultimately determine your program. Simply adopting a program because others are doing it or because it seems inherently good may be a tactical error.

2. *Process competence must be grown organically.* Effective process improvement programs cannot be bought off the shelf.[7] Improvement work should be viewed as an evolutionary spiral that is adjusted and retooled along the way. It's best to start small and realistically with a goal to build competence and commitment. As demonstrated competencies grow, expectations can be increased and more complex issues can be tackled. Supporting methodologies and infrastructures can be adjusted dynamically to remain aligned with improvement needs as well. While it may be useful to tackle the proverbial low-hanging fruit in the early stages, it is important to remember that skill and effort requirements will increase significantly as we move toward more complex challenges.

3. *Heroes kill process.* Substantial improvement in performance outcomes involves changing how business outcomes are obtained. Frequently, when confronted with the need to improve, we simply continue to apply old methods, just with more intensity. Individual heroes or SWAT teams attack problems quickly and with great focus in response to the fix-it-now mandate. Heroics that apply extensions of past approaches to problem solving have several key drawbacks. First, they generally don't apply the rigor required to understand causation or to deploy effective solutions. Second, they send a powerful signal that reinforces previous paradigms, and third, they extend rugged individualism instead of promoting cross-functional cooperation. Perhaps most importantly though, heroes tend to think and understand at the local level, instead of at the system level, and as discussed earlier, solutions derived at the local level may suboptimize the system.

Whereas heroes are highly valued in the traditional organization, they can be counterproductive in a process-focused organization. Heroes have a cherished bias for action. That is, they don't waste valuable time investigating causation, they are unimpeded by methodology, and they take decisive action. Results are fast—or so we think. The process-focused organization replaces the hero with the team player and the art of heroics with structured methods and systems thinking.

4. *Sustained change must be self-sustaining.* Research has shown that change occurs naturally at the system periphery where people are working from within the context of their localized roles.[8] Many performance improvement efforts ignore this reality and seek to impose directed change. While it is necessary to utilize management push in the early stages of a change program, push has severe limitations and is unable to sustain change over the long term. The ultimate objective is to attain a self-sustaining state, where complex challenges are tackled by competent and intrinsically motivated employees. This state can only be attained when employee pull is the

operative sustaining force.[9] A key challenge for change leaders is to enable the natural forces of change while aligning them with the enterprise vision.

5. *Local optima do not equal system improvement.* As discussed previously, improvements to system components may not improve system-level performance. This is one of the reasons why we may see flat or worsening organizational performance while at the same time numerous improvements are being reported. The lesson is that all improvement should be planned and evaluated in terms of the broader system (in other words, the business enterprise).

6. *Activity does not translate to results.* Process improvement programs sometimes suffer a means/ends inversion—where the primary emphasis is placed on activity, not results. Although we certainly can't grow competency or produce results without activity, it's important to keep our sights on the real performance measure—business results. An emphasis on activity can promote high levels of attention to unimportant areas and can promote a cosmetic culture where looking busy is more valued than producing real results. Process improvement requires a significant investment of valuable time and resources. Therefore, it is important to target our investments in areas and ways that offer a meaningful economic return. When a process is viewed in economic terms, it may actually make more sense to leave it alone or outsource it than to improve it.[10]

7. *Not everything is a nail.* As stated previously, it's not uncommon to see an organization acquire a methodology and then try to apply it to every problem in sight. Methodology, like any tool, should be carefully configured to reflect the unique needs of the organization and the specific problems being addressed. Methodology selection should be driven by an honest assessment of improvement needs. Factors to consider when selecting or configuring process improvement methods may include: (1) the nature and magnitude of the improvement required, (2) the time available to gain the improvement, (3) organizational competence in process work, and (4) the degree of risk that is acceptable.

There are significant differences between the methodologies that comprise the contemporary process tool kit. Six Sigma, for example, focuses on process capability and quality, while lean principles focus on efficiency. Six Sigma is a reductionalistic approach that seeks to identify causation of defects, while lean principles reflect more of a systems perspective via their focus on value streams and flow. Both approaches more or less restrict their focus to process issues. In contrast, reengineering is a more holistic approach that includes organizational structures and systems in combination with process. Reengineering remains the big-bang approach to process work.

The key lesson here is that if we don't carefully consider methodology and tool selection when launching improvement projects, our efforts have less chance of success.

8. *Too much analysis can lead to paralysis.* Effectively solving performance problems requires that we identify and understand relevant problems, that we discover their root causes, and that we design and deploy solutions that resolve the causes. The degree of complexity and risk associated with these steps can vary substantially—from as obvious as the nose on our face to the proverbial needle in the haystack. Increasing levels of complexity warrant increased levels of rigor to mitigate the risks associated with complexity. The problem is, while rigor is the key safeguard, not all problems require equal levels of rigor. The practical challenge we face is how to apply the level of rigor that appropriately balances solution speed and risks. A key to avoiding analysis paralysis is to learn how to effectively tailor improvement methodologies to match the unique needs and circumstances of projects. Again, one size does not fit all.

9. *How long depends on how much.* We frequently receive conflicting advice about how to scope and schedule improvement projects. This is where many improvement programs stumble. Sometimes we are advised to schedule project time lines around some fixed time frame, and at the same time we are advised to scope projects so they will produce meaningful business results. In reality, the time it takes depends on how much we're trying to accomplish.

Improvement projects are the engine of change, so it's essential to plan them realistically. Both duration and scope must be carefully considered when planning, supporting, and evaluating projects. Simple problems generally require simple solutions and short time lines. Complex problems generally require more sophisticated tools and longer time lines.

The improvement half-life concept provides useful perspective regarding the time required to improve process performance. Arthur Schneiderman found that any defect level that is subjected to continuous improvement will improve at a constant rate that is characterized by the improvement half-life (the time required to reduce defects by 50 percent).[11] Based on this finding, we can expect to attain 50 percent of the targeted improvement during the half-life interval, with 50 percent of the remaining gap taking an additional half-life, and so on. The time duration of the half-life is related to the technical and organizational complexity of a process. Technical complexity relates to the lead time of the process, the ability to conduct effective experiments, and the degree of technical know-how that is involved. Organizational complexity refers to the number and types of people from different organizational functions that are required to carry out the improvement.[12]

Schneiderman determined that processes characterized by high organizational complexity have half-lives ranging from 14 to 22 months (depending on the corresponding degree of technical complexity).

The half-life concept is important to us for two reasons. First, since business processes generally have high degrees of organizational complexity, their half-lives will be long. This means we should adjust our expectations appropriately. Second, the initial improvement round will generally be the easiest. This means we must adjust our expectations after the "low-hanging fruit" has been picked.

10. *Crossing the goal line doesn't always score.* It's not uncommon to see improvement efforts fail to reach their potential because solutions don't become sufficiently institutionalized. Sometimes, project teams are so anxious to finish projects or management is so anxious to harvest the benefits, that the deployment of solutions is not effectively planned or executed. In other instances, teams may develop effective deployment plans, but the organization fails to embrace the changes. Project teams come and go and can't be accountable for the long-term results. As W. Edwards Deming used to remind us, the system of production is owned by management. Only management can be held accountable for ensuring the proposed changes are deployed and managed. Unfortunately, many performance improvement programs fail to sufficiently engage enterprise management. To sustain process improvement results, our business processes must be managed by the same executives who manage our enterprises.

This chapter discussed the limitations of the existing process paradigm, the inherent weaknesses of the functional design, a few lessons from systems theory, and the laws of process work. The operating models, strategies, and systems described in later chapters build on these lessons and principles to guide the transition to process focus.

3
Clarifying Process

THE POWER OF PROCESS

Figure 3.1 illustrates the basic building blocks of organizational design. Individually, each component determines a particular characteristic of the organization. Combined, they determine how effectively the organization operates as a system. What's important to note is the central role played by the concept of process in linking these components.

Consider leadership. Leadership deals with establishing direction and goals, deploying action plans to reach these goals, and maintaining ongoing organizational alignment with goals. Aren't these accomplished by process? Also, organizations design organizational structures and systems to manage the resources that perform the work of the enterprise. Since this work, in aggregate, is actually process work, shouldn't the structures and systems be designed to support effective process operations? If we really think about it, process is what gives organizational structures and systems meaning, and should shape their design and operation. Process also shapes job designs, accountabilities, and skill requirements—all of which significantly impact culture and competencies.

These points combine to support the assertion that process provides us with a powerful lever for improving and managing enterprise performance. Processes are the glue that links and aligns the mosaic of organizational subsystems into a coherent whole. Moreover, processes are unique in that they, more than any other component, have the ability to align and manage the other building blocks so that each contributes to the performance of the total system. *This, it seems to me, is the real power of process.*

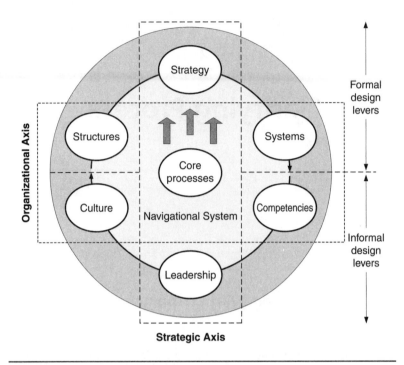

Organizational Axis

Figure 3.1   Process as the linchpin to organizational performance.

Adapted from Robert H. Miles, *Leading Corporate Transformation* (San Francisco: Jossey-Bass, 1997): 37.

DEFINING PROCESSES

Since this is a book about process, it is appropriate that we work from a shared definition of the concept. Michael Hammer provides an excellent definition and commentary regarding process in *The Agenda*. Hammer defines process as "an organized group of related activities that work together to transform one or more kinds of input into outputs that are of value to the customer." This definition communicates several key points. First, a process is a group of activities, not just one. Second, the activities comprising a process are not random or ad hoc, they are related and organized. Third, all the activities in a process must work together toward a common goal. And fourth, processes exist to create a result the customers care about.[1] These customers can be internal or external to the organization. Figure 3.2 illustrates a simple process model.

A process can also be viewed as a value chain, where each activity, or step, contributes to the end result. Some of these activities directly contribute

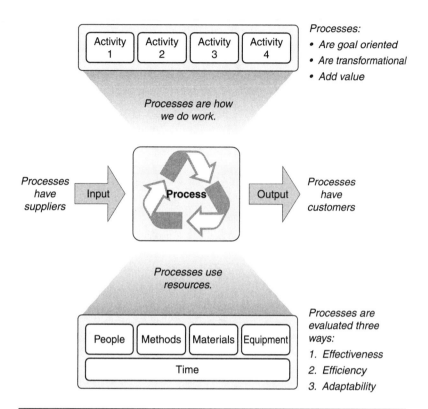

Figure 3.2   A simple process model. A process is collection of actions and resources that work together to transform one or more kinds of input into outputs that are of value to the customer.

value, while others may not. All activities consume enterprise resources, however. A challenge for management is to discover how to eliminate steps that do not add value and to improve the efficiency of those that do. Later, we will discuss how to use activity-based costing (ABC) techniques to generate the data required to tackle this challenge.

TYPES OF PROCESSES

Organizations use different types of processes to conduct the work of the enterprise. Figure 3.3 illustrates three principal types of processes along with examples of each type.[2] The following narrative provides additional amplification.

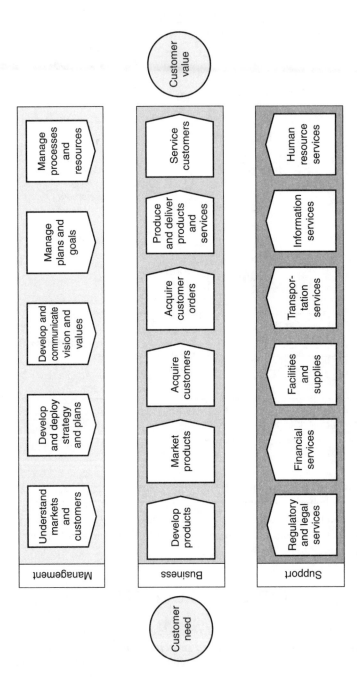

Figure 3.3 Types of enterprise processes.

a. *Management processes.* These are the processes used to provide direction and governance for the enterprise. They are generally conducted by senior leaders to set organizational goals, develop and deploy strategy to attain goals, establish and manage organization designs, and manage performance to goals. Management processes also shape and manage the business and support processes used by the enterprise.

b. *Business processes.* These are the processes that reflect the unique competencies of the enterprise and are mission critical. They tend to lie on or close to the value creation stream and are the processes that are seen and experienced by external customers. Value-creating business processes begin and end with the external customer, tend to be large in scope, and commonly span multiple organizational components. While organizations may have hundreds of work processes, they usually have very few business processes (five to seven are typical). Since this group of processes represents the core competencies of the organization, it should be the primary focus of our performance improvement work.

c. *Support processes.* Support processes exist to support the apparatus of the enterprise. Since the support needs of business organizations are similar, these processes tend to be fairly standardized and are frequent candidates for outsourcing. The customers of support processes are internal to the organization.

It should be clear that while these three categories play significantly different roles, they must be aligned and integrated to enable effective performance of the total system. The implication of this observation is that effective and sustained performance improvement must consider the management and support processes as well as the core business processes.

PROCESS CONCEPTS

Before venturing too far into the world of process, it is important that we establish a few foundation concepts. Although these concepts are relatively simple, experience has shown that they can be the source of confusion if not clearly understood.

a. *The use of time.* As individual work objects (products or services) move through processes, there are times when they are being worked on and there are times they're not being worked on. When an object is not being worked on, that is, when it's just sitting somewhere waiting, the time associated with this interval is called *idle time.* When the object is being worked on, that is, when resources are being consumed in the performance of work, this time is called *process time*. When we combine the various increments of idle and process time, we have the time it takes the work object to travel through the end-to-end process. This end-to-end time is called *lead time* and may be represented by the following equation:

$$LT = \sum T_{PT} + \sum T_{IT}$$

Note: While some practitioners refer to the end-to-end time as cycle time, we use the term cycle time to describe the cyclic rate at which a process produces outcomes.

As mentioned previously, lead time is a customer-experienced phenomenon that plays a significant role in determining organizational responsiveness to market conditions. When we examine business processes, we generally find that the process time component occupies a small fraction of the lead time. I once worked on an insurance process that required over three weeks of lead time, while the process time involved only 23 minutes. In this case, which is not at all uncommon, the insurance applications sat around 99.7 percent of the available work time collecting dust, cost, and risk. The strategy for reducing lead time in these circumstances is straightforward—eliminate the idle time.

Figure 3.4 illustrates these time-related concepts graphically.

b. *The value contribution of work.* As just mentioned, process time is the time that resources are being consumed in the performance of work. While all work activities consume resources, not all work contributes equally to value creation. To differentiate the relative importance of work, it is helpful to classify work activities in terms of the degree to which they contribute to value creation. Although various classification schemes are used, most divide work into three categories: (1) work that adds value, (2) work that enables value, and (3) waste work. Value-adding work (VA) is work that changes the state or form of the product or service in a way the customer values and is willing to pay for. Value-enabling work (VE) does not add customer value, but is required to enable the work that does. Examples of VE include maintaining controls, performing checks, and coordinating work. Since VE is required, it generally cannot be removed without changing the process design. Waste work (WW) is work that neither adds nor enables value. Examples of WW include rechecking, following up, and some approvals. We can usually remove WW without adversely impacting process performance. The total process time may be represented by the following equation:

$$PT = \sum PT_{VA} + \sum PT_{VE} + \sum PT_{WW}$$

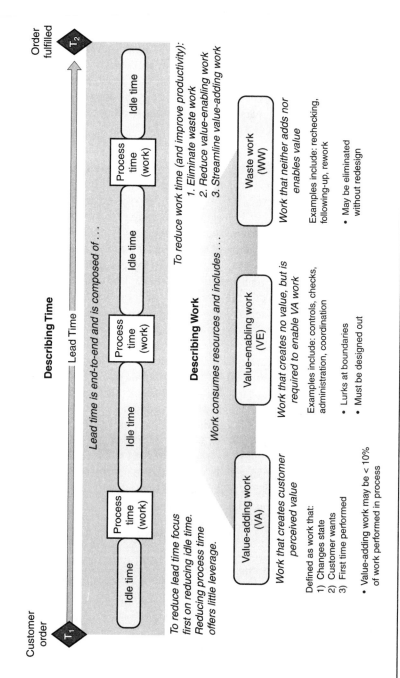

Figure 3.4 Describing process time and work concepts.

When we examine business processes, we generally find that the VA component (PT_{VA}) accounts for a relatively small percentage of the total effort applied (commonly around the 20 percent to 30 percent range). This means that most of the resources consumed by our processes are consumed for non-value-adding work (PT_{VE} and PT_{WW}). This predictable relationship guides our strategies for improving the productivity of our processes—which is first to focus on eliminating the WW, second to reduce the VE, and third, to improve the efficiency of VA.

c. *The enemy called variation.* Variation is the bane of process. The goal of processes is to reliably produce outcomes that are within predetermined ranges. Excessive or uncontrolled variation undermines this goal, as well as drives poor quality, generates waste, and imposes costly overhead to detect, correct, or service quality problems. Variation is a key source of the "hidden factory" that burdens most enterprises today.

Quality professionals have long used the *cost of quality* concept as a way to quantify the adverse impact of poor quality by using the language of business (dollars). The common approach is to capture quality-related costs via four categories: (1) prevention costs, (2) appraisal costs, (3) internal failure costs, and (4) external failure costs. What practitioners have found is that, when combined, these four categories frequently represent between 15 percent and 25 percent of the total cost of production.[3] While it is apparent that failure costs are clearly linked to variation, prevention and appraisal costs are also determined, in part, by variation. After all, if a process exhibits no variation, its results would be absolutely repeatable and there would be no reason to incur prevention or appraisal costs. We know, however, that all processes exhibit variation.

In process work we recognize two types of variation. The first is called *common cause* variation and the second is called *special cause* variation. Common cause variation can be viewed as the general background noise that occurs in any system. It is a natural byproduct of the process design and is normally distributed (that is, it aligns with the normal curve). Figure 3.5 illustrates common cause variation and how it reflects normality. Common cause variation determines the capability of our processes, as long as there is no special cause variation operating in the process. Unlike common cause variation, special cause variation is not a natural part of the system. It is driven by external or intermittent causes that destabilize the process and make it unpredictable (that is, it no longer aligns with the normal curve). When this occurs, the process is said to be out of control (which means the process is no longer operating within the normal distribution). Figure 3.6 illustrates examples of special cause variation.

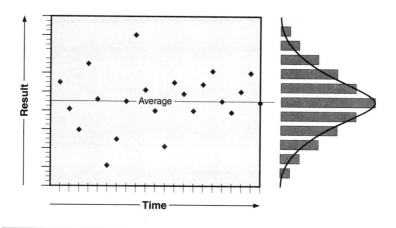

Figure 3.5 Common cause variation.

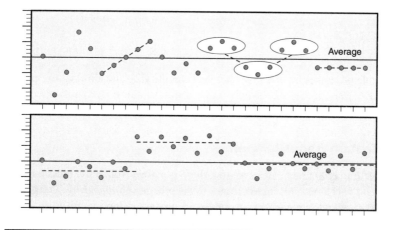

Figure 3.6 Special cause variation.

This leads us to the concept of process capability. A capable process is simply a process that is able to consistently produce a desired result. When described in terms of variation, this means: (1) there is no special cause variation present, and (2) the common cause variation that is present operates within acceptable tolerances. Figure 3.7 illustrates a capable process. It's important to note that an out of control process cannot be considered capable, regardless of the outcomes it produces. The strategy for maintaining

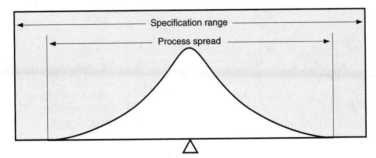

Capable processes:
- Do not produce nonconformances
- Reduce waste and rework
- Increase capacity
- Require less inspection
- Are in control

Figure 3.7   Describing process capability—variation determines the capability of processes.

capable processes involves two steps: (1) identifying and eliminating special cause variation and (2) keeping the common cause variation operating within acceptable levels.

A Caution About Tampering

While it may not be obvious at first, there is a powerful lesson hidden in the topic of variation. This lesson relates to the practice of *tampering*. Tampering refers to situations where fluctuations in process behaviors resulting from common cause variation are interpreted as resulting from special causes and process adjustments are implemented in an effort to correct the process. When this occurs, efforts to improve process behavior actually increase process variation, instead of decreasing it. This additional variation will likely fuel additional corrections to compensate for previous corrections, eventually producing a situation where the process spirals out of control. The lesson here is that we must understand what we are observing (common or special cause) before we react to it. As business managers we are proud of our bias toward action; however, in process work, action can be, and frequently is, worse than no action.

COST-RELATED CONCEPTS

Why is it that we sometimes see reported results that never seem to materialize on the bottom line? From my experience, the answer frequently has a lot to do with how we measure and manage savings. Using the following classification scheme when measuring and reporting savings provides a more accurate picture of our accomplishments:

a. *Hard dollar savings.* Hard dollar savings describes real reductions in operating expense. This means that your organization will be writing fewer checks or making larger deposits because of an improvement. Management should expect to see hard dollar savings impact the bottom line within a reasonable time frame. If it doesn't, then the reported savings are not hard dollar savings.

b. *Soft dollar savings.* Soft dollar savings describes potential reductions in operating expense or increased revenues. For example, when work is removed from a process without eliminating resources, the resulting improvement is actually freed capacity. This capacity is expressed as a soft savings since it reflects a potential benefit. Of course, this capacity must eventually be utilized in some useful way or the improvement is irrelevant. The lesson here is that soft savings must be actively tracked and managed to ensure they eventually become relevant, that is, they eventually become hard dollar savings. Effectively managing this category is one of the key practical challenges facing improvement programs and is a significant contributor to the process paradox.

c. *Intangible savings.* Intangible savings describes the factors that are too subjective to quantify in dollars. Examples might include customer satisfaction, customer loyalty, or competitive advantage. The fact that intangible improvements are difficult to express in dollars does not make them less important. Frequently, intangible improvements provide powerful opportunities for increasing value delivered.

Using these categories to report improvement results provides a more accurate representation of our improvement efforts. This helps avoid creating false expectations and clarifies the need to manage the soft and intangible categories if we are to translate them into meaningful outcomes. My experience has been that most reported savings actually fall into the soft category and that they fail to complete the journey to the hard dollar savings category because we don't actively manage them once they are reported.

4

Connecting Process and Organization

THE PROCESS ORGANIZATION

There is an alternative organizational form that recognizes the integrative and aligning nature of process. This organization is known as the process-focused organization (or PFO). Process-focused organizations differ from traditional organizations in several key ways. First, they design and manage end-to-end processes rather than tasks. Second, they measure process level results instead of departmental efficiencies. And third, they think in terms of customer goals instead of localized functional goals. These differences combine to create an organization that is more focused on, aligned with, and responsive to the needs of its value-creating processes.[1] The PFO offers a more powerful and complete paradigm for exploiting the power of process.

Figure 4.1 illustrates a PFO. The differences between the functional and process organization are subtle, but profound. Whereas functions are the key organizing element in the functional organization, process takes precedence in the PFO. Functions still exist in the PFO, but they exist for a different reason—to meet the needs of the value-creating business processes.

Two key features of the PFO are readily visible in Figure 4.1. First, there is a new role, called the *process owner,* and, second, enterprise goals and resources are deployed to functions via processes. This ensures that functions are fully aligned with and capable of meeting the needs of the processes they support.

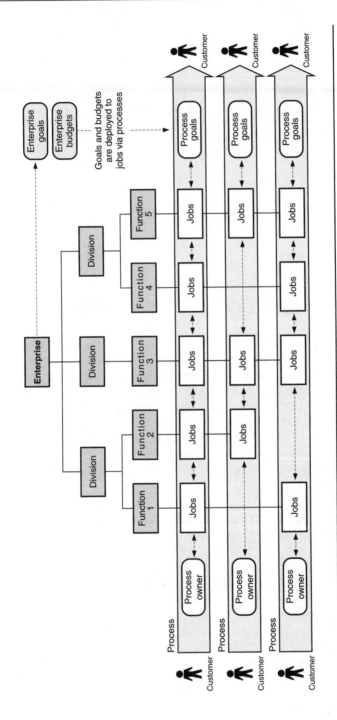

Figure 4.1   The process-focused organization.

Two other key features are not visible on the diagram. The first involves the separation of process design from process execution and the second involves performance measurement. In the PFO, managerial responsibility is split—with process owners being responsible for the process designs and functional managers being responsible for executing the processes as designed.[2] Performance is primarily evaluated in terms of process performance, not functional efficiency. In the PFO, jobs tend to be broader in scope, authority is moved closer to the front lines, and work-related communications travel horizontally. Since workflow coordination is a process matter, and the PFO is designed to manage processes, there is less need for multiple layers of management to coordinate work in the PFO.

The PFO expands individual responsibility and requires greater intergroup cooperation than the functional organization. By promoting broad organizational alignment to business processes, however, the PFO reduces the opportunity for the organizational friction that comes from self-interest, and promotes intergroup cooperation.

Linking the PFO to the Performance Challenges

Earlier, we talked about the challenges faced by business enterprises. Now that we've introduced the PFO, let's see if it has the potential to positively address these challenges:

a. *Speed.* We are challenged to decrease the time it takes to design, produce, and deliver products and services. Since the PFO focuses on end-to-end process performance, issues of time and speed are apparent and can be managed. Whereas the functional organization is not concerned with end-to-end time and speed, the PFO relies on it.

b. *Waste.* We are challenged to decrease waste. Performing work that does not add value or performing work more than once is wasteful. In the traditional organization we are able to reduce waste at the local level in the hope that it will improve overall organizational efficiency. But, as we've seen, local efficiency improvements may actually degrade enterprise efficiency. By exposing the interdependencies that exist across our processes, the PFO helps us understand the impacts of local changes on dependent units and the value stream as a whole. Perhaps more importantly, customer value creation is a concept that applies to business processes, not to functional units.

c. *Quality.* Quality is a customer-focused concept that considers the customer experience along the value chain as well as the product or service that is delivered at the end of the chain. By organizing and measuring performance in terms of the value-creating business processes, where each process directly impacts customers, the PFO ensures a focus on customer-perceived quality. Apart from knowing what quality is, another challenge is to learn how to prevent defects, rather than detecting and correcting them. The traditional method of postprocess inspection has proven to be both ineffective and costly. By focusing on the end-to-end process, the PFO sets the stage for process management techniques that are not always possible in the traditional organization.

d. *Alignment.* We are challenged to improve and sustain the alignment of the components that comprise our organizations so that everyone is contributing to enterprise-level performance. The PFO addresses the alignment challenge by first aligning the key business processes to enterprise goals and strategies, and then aligning the apparatus of the organization (structures, systems, and resources) to meet process needs. Local concerns are relevant only to the degree that they impact process performance, not local efficiency.

e. *Manageability.* We are challenged to do a better job of managing the connections between the functions that comprise our cross-functional processes and to manage outcomes more proactively. Since the contemporary organization is designed to manage functions vertically, however, it has little visibility to the relationships between functions. In contrast, by giving primacy to the horizontal dimension, the PFO manages the relationships between the functions as well as the functions themselves.

f. *Adaptability.* The traditional approach to planning has proven to be a less effective strategy than the ability to quickly adapt to change. Effective adaptability involves several organizational capabilities, including knowing when to change, what to change to, how to change, and how to sustain change. Although the traditional organization is able to know when a result must change, it is not very effective at knowing what must be changed to effectively produce the result. This is due, in part, to the fact that while the traditional organization is able to understand and manage the parts, it is not so good at understanding or managing the whole (that is, the end-to-end system). The PFO, on the other hand, gives us visibility into the full end-to-end system of value creation and maintains clear connections between internal capabilities and final outcomes. By making cause-and-effect directly observable and manageable, the PFO is better able to deploy and sustain change.

THE BUILDING BLOCKS TO BECOMING A PROCESS-FOCUSED ORGANIZATION

Becoming a PFO involves significant changes in our approach to organizational management. The most significant change is that organizational leaders must start thinking horizontally as well as vertically. This relatively simple notion is more challenging than one might expect, because most of what we do and have learned is vertically aligned—including how we develop and deploy goals and budgets, and how we manage performance and recognition, to name just a few. It is essential that management acknowledge the relevance of managing the horizontal dimension before considering the journey to process focus. This is not the same as embracing process improvement. *Becoming a PFO involves much more than simply improving processes—it extends the challenge to learning how to manage organizational performance via process.* The key caution is: as long as your management views performance as a vertical issue, your organization is not ready for process focus.

It is important to note that organizations with process improvement programs are not necessarily process-focused organizations, nor are they necessarily on the path to becoming process-focused. To the extent that these programs reflect the current process paradigm, they are distracted from the vision of the process-focused organization.

It's equally important to point out that there is no set way to achieve process focus, nor is there one best way to design your organizational structures and systems to support processes. However, regardless of how you get there, or how you look once you get there, the fundamental building blocks for achieving process focus are the same.

Build on Value-Creating Processes

The fundamental building block of the PFO is the small family of processes that creates value for your customers. These are the processes to which we want to align our organizational structures and systems.

The first step toward process focus involves developing a clear understanding of the enterprise's value proposition. This is an absolute and will be the basis for all that follows. The next step is to identify the business processes that drive value creation. These are generally processes that directly touch your products, services, or customers. This group of processes describes the core competency of the enterprise and is a key determinant of business success.

After we've identified our value-creating processes, we want to evaluate their health. This evaluation lays the foundation for our process improvement and process management strategies going forward. The improvement strategy is to focus first on our value-creating processes that are underperforming, while the management strategy is to learn how to effectively manage the family of value-creating processes.

Deploy Strategy via Process

Traditional strategy deployment approaches deploy strategy, goals, and plans to organizations through a downward system of decomposition. This makes perfectly good sense, that is, until we consider how the approach adversely impacts culture and performance. First, vertical decomposition affirms the primacy of the functional silo and fuels the belief that performance is judged solely by those above us, not by our customers. Second, vertical decomposition can (and frequently does) promote organizational misalignment since there is nothing that causes functional unit goals and plans to be aligned horizontally, along the flow of value creation. This approach can result in functional unit goals that have little positive relationship to enterprise performance. This is one reason we frequently see success without achievement in functional organizations.

Geary Rummler and Alan Brache offer an approach to strategy deployment that recognizes the needs of both the horizontal and vertical dimensions of performance management.[3] Their idea is simple and powerful. Instead of deploying enterprise strategy and goals downward through organizational silos, deploy them horizontally through business processes and then aggregate them upwardly through the silos. Figure 4.2 illustrates the concept. As you can see, functional units still have goals with this approach, however, they are now aligned with the processes they support, not the silos in which they reside. The real power of this approach is that it enables us to manage the vertical and horizontal performance dimensions simultaneously via integrated performance criteria. So it's not one or the other, it's both.

Design Jobs to Support Process, Not Silos

Traditionally, jobs are designed to support the needs of the functional units in which they reside. As a consequence, jobs are commonly designed to support vertically aligned goals, not the needs of the cross-functional processes they support. This generally results in job designs that seek to maximize localized efficiency. Eliyahu Goldratt teaches us valuable lessons about the potential adverse effects of localized efficiency in *The Goal*.[4]

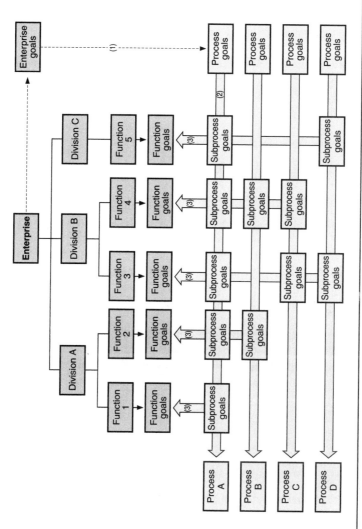

Figure 4.2 Enterprise goal deployment in a process-focused organization.

Designing jobs to support processes begins with understanding the flow of value, the product and service transitions that occur along the flow of value, and the interdependencies that exist between the functional units participating in these transitions. This understanding begins with value stream mapping.

A few years back, the internal customer concept was emphasized as a means to understand the interdependencies between functional units. The problem with this approach is that downstream customers base their requirements on localized perspectives, not the full cross-functional perspective required to understand what adds value and what doesn't. Value stream mapping of end-to-end business processes provides this perspective.

The challenge is to learn how to design jobs to enable the processes they support while they continue to be managed vertically. The solution to this challenge is the two-dimensional approach described in Figure 4.2.

Deploy Resources via Process

Budget is the currency of the internal economy. Budget not only determines the resources that are made available to perform daily process work, it also determines which projects will be launched today to impact future capabilities or outcomes. Unfortunately, budget planning, like strategy, typically fails to incorporate process. In traditional budgeting work, subordinate units are asked to identify the resources they require to sustain themselves and drive action plans during the planning period. Budgets are then upwardly aggregated through silos.

Since there are no clear connections to the economies of the value-creating processes, budgeting becomes a survival game where the objective is to protect the interest of the functional unit. In good times, funds flow freely to those who are best at asking. In lean times, budgets are squeezed irrespective of process needs or strategies, thereby eliminating mission-critical resources in some areas, while other areas are unhurt. It stands to reason that budgeting should be connected to managing and improving enterprise performance, and that process is the most suitable organizing principle.

Manage Performance via Process, Not Silos

In traditional organizations, the primacy of the hierarchy promotes vertically aligned measurements, typically resulting in localized efficiency as the primary measurement concern. But we've already seen how localized efficiency has little to do with the health of the broader process and how it can actually suboptimize overall process performance.

Since the process organization recognizes the primacy of process, it focuses on managing its value-creating processes as the primary measurement concern. In its simplest form, process management involves just three steps: (1) establish process goals that reflect enterprise performance requirements, (2) establish process-level measurements that reflect performance relative to goals, and (3) compare measurement results with goals to determine if corrective action is required. Of course, process goals must be translated to the functional units that support them to ensure alignment between unit and process performance management. We will discuss process measurement and control in greater detail in chapter 12.

Part II

Becoming a Process Organization

Part II introduces an approach for transitioning a functionally managed organization to a process-focused organization. The approach is designed to establish the operating structures necessary to manage and continuously improve key cross-functional business processes, while ensuring continued alignment between those processes and key business drivers, strategies, and goals. It utilizes process improvement and process management as key enablers, but not as the overarching management framework. The approach is built around three principal components: (1) an operating model that describes the key operating structures and relationships, (2) a process improvement road map to guide process work, and (3) an implementation pathway to guide the transformation process.

Part II includes two chapters. The first, chapter 5, introduces an operational model that serves as the foundation for the PFO. The model identifies the key structures and roles that enable PFO operations. Chapter 6 introduces the Process Improvement Road Map. The road map is designed to sequence process work so that we systematically evolve the maturity of our business processes. Part III assimilates these ideas into a strategy for guiding the transformation to a process-focused organization.

REQUIREMENTS OF ORGANIZATIONAL CHANGE

The journey to becoming a PFO involves fundamental organizational change. Even when all of the conditions are favorable, change of this magnitude is a highly complex and risky undertaking. Personal experience and observation has shown that organizational change programs tend to begin with a burst of enthusiasm and then quietly wind down after two to three years. This pattern seems to be affirmed by a recent survey regarding Six Sigma programs.[1]

The approach outlined in this book seeks to reduce change complexity and risk in two ways. First, the implementation pathway is composed of phases that are relatively small (in terms of effort) and narrowly focused (in terms of scope). These phases are designed to be executed sequentially, thereby making implementation less complex and more manageable. Second, the pathway incorporates mechanisms that are explicitly designed to address the needs of large-scale change. When considering large-scale change, it is essential to remember the following:

1. *Change requires shared vision.* Shared vision fuels the tension required to inspire action and to provide the constancy required to align efforts over time. Beginning a change effort without shared vision is risky, since the various stakeholders may be working from entirely different agendas. Moreover, without tension, there is little motivation or incentive to pursue change. The transformation strategy approach seeds the enterprise-level vision by suggesting an end-state operating model and fuels tension by conducting an assessment of enterprise and process performance relative to expectations.

2. *Change requires a viable plan.* A change plan must be carefully crafted and adjusted as appropriate to keep the vision in focus. The transformation strategy approach provides a high-level implementation plan for attaining process focus. All of the steps in the plan have a purpose, so skipping or short-circuiting them will almost certainly result in problems later. If your management fails to fully understand and embrace both the vision and plan, your chances of success are significantly reduced.

3. *Change requires engaged leadership.* Planned change requires leadership that is knowledgeable, committed, and involved. Knowledgeable leadership has a clear understanding of the goals and plans of the change effort, as well as the principles of organizational change. Without this knowledge, leaders cannot be effective. Committed leadership believes in the importance of the change effort and is resolute in its support of it. Involved leadership spends its time actively engaged in the initiative. Engaged leaders signal change through their behaviors and actions, whereas disengaged leaders continue pulling the same organizational levers as before (sending contradictory messages through the organization). The transformation strategy approach provides mechanisms for actively engaging enterprise leaders throughout the entire change process.

We've all heard the definition of insanity as doing things the same way while expecting different results. This applies to change as well. As practitioners we must *ensure that we don't enable the status quo.* Ownership for organizational change can only rest in one place—on the shoulders of enterprise leaders. Having supporting cast members doing the work of leaders disengages the leaders and is counterproductive to the initiative, regardless of our motives or arguments. This is a common tactical error on the part of support practitioners.

The operating paradigms of the PFO can be challenging to people who grew up in hierarchical organizations. Many of the styles, beliefs, and politics that were appropriate in the vertically oriented world will not be as highly valued in the horizontally oriented world. There will be a natural tendency to retain old values or to resist new values. It's essential that leaders and practitioners accept this reality and be prepared to deal with it openly and honestly. Denial may ease the immediate discomfort, but can be very harmful over the long run.

The importance of these challenges cannot be overemphasized too strongly. The failure to understand and address the dynamics of change will greatly reduce chances of success. Therefore, practitioners and leaders are urged to carefully and continuously consider these dynamics throughout the lifecycle of the initiative.

5

Introducing an Operational Model for the PFO

The PFO operating model includes five key components (see Figure 5.1). The roles and responsibilities associated with each component are described in the following narrative.

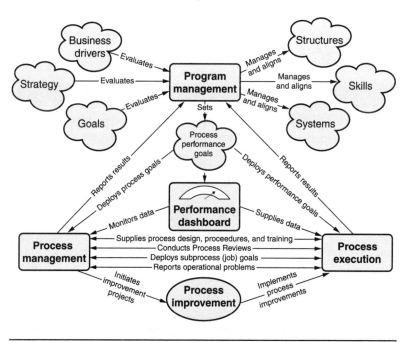

Figure 5.1 A process-focused organization systems model.

MODEL DESCRIPTION

Program Management Component

Program management provides the leadership engine for the journey to process focus. This is where senior management evaluates key business drivers, strategies, and goals to set and maintain process performance goals; evaluates performance relative to those goals; and maintains alignment between processes and organizational structures, skills, and systems. We use the process council as the primary vehicle for engaging senior managers in program management work. The roles and responsibilities associated with program management include:

> *Process council.* Comprised of executive managers (with the CEO as leader)

- Initial responsibilities:
  - Sets and communicates program-level objectives and strategies.
  - Determines priority processes and sets performance expectations.
  - Establishes process owners for priority processes.
- Ongoing responsibilities:
  - Manages program-level plans and accountabilities.
  - Monitors priority process performance (via feedback systems).
  - Sets and deploys enterprise strategy and budgets via core processes.
  - Aligns organizational structures and systems with core processes.
  - Aligns performance management systems with core processes.

Process Management Component

Process management is concerned with providing and enabling a process design that is capable of meeting the performance goals set by program management. Process management owns the design of the process, but not the execution of process work. Process execution is still managed by functional managers.

There are two key roles associated with the process management component—the process owner and the process management team. The process owner is a senior manager who has primary accountability for designing and enabling a capable process. The process management team includes representatives from the functional units (for example, departments) that participate in the process. The process owner serves as the team leader for the process management team and as a member of the process council.

Process owner. A senior executive (and member of the process council)

- Responsibilities:

  - Deploys strategic process plans to functional units participating in process.

  - Sets process budget and deploys to functional units.

  - Resolves cross-process conflicts (with other owners).

Process management team. A permanent cross-functional team including representatives from functions participating in process. The process owner is the team leader.

- Responsibilities:

  - Develops and maintains process design, procedures, and training.

  - Develops and maintains process performance management system (including performance dimensions, goals, and measurements).

  - Monitors process performance (via performance management system) and charters process improvement projects as appropriate.

  - Conducts process training and audits as required.

Process Execution Component

Process execution manages the execution of processes and the resources required to perform them. Generally, this component is organized by functional units (for example, departments or sections) and is responsible for:

(1) ensuring compliance with process design, (2) building employee skills and knowledge, and (3) collecting and reporting process performance and resource utilization data. The key roles and responsibilities associated with this component include:

> *Functional managers.* Senior managers of the functional units participating in the business process.

> - Responsibilities:
>   - Develops and executes work plans in support of process goals and plans.
>   - Follows operating budgets deployed via core processes.
>   - Trains and coaches supervisors in coaching skills.

> *Supervisors (Coaches).* Frontline supervisors within the functions participating in the business processes.

> - Responsibilities:
>   - Balances resources within functional units.
>   - Coaches and develops process performers.
>   - Advises process team representative of operational difficulties.

> *Process performers.* Frontline employees performing the process.

> - Responsibilities:
>   - Executes processes in accordance with documented procedures.
>   - Advises process team representative of operational difficulties.

Process Improvement Component

Process improvement is positioned as the engine of change. Improvement activities are generally project-based initiatives that use structured analysis and design tools to identify and implement solutions to process problems. Process improvement projects are championed by process owners. Since the process owners are ultimately responsible for the success of projects, it is essential that they take an active role in providing the required resources and clearing obstacles encountered by teams. The process owners should provide regular updates to the process council regarding the projects underway.

Project champion. An executive with sufficient authority to support the process improvement project (usually filled by the process owner).

- Responsibilities:
    - Initiates projects and team formation.
    - Provides training and other support required to prepare and enable teams.
    - Clears obstacles to team performance.
    - Reports project status to process council.

Project coach. An individual who is highly skilled in team and process improvement methods. Usually an internal consultative resource and not a team member.

- Responsibilities:
    - Facilitates team development and project execution using appropriate methodologies and tools.
    - Keeps project champion informed regarding team issues, risks, or needs.

Project team. Teams are temporary organizations that form to conduct specific projects. All members are equally committed to and responsible for delivered outcomes.

- Responsibilities:
    - Charters projects designed to attain project goals.
    - Conducts projects using defined project plans and methodologies appropriate to project goals.
    - Maintains project plans and provides regular updates to project champion.

Performance Dashboard

The purpose of the dashboard is to establish meaningful linkages between business outcomes and process performance. By establishing process performance measures that are linked to business outcomes, the dashboard provides a means to manage outcomes by managing the drivers of those outcomes. The process council may designate a dashboard coordinator to manage the technical aspects of data collection, storage, analysis, and reporting. The implementation strategy includes guidance for designing and deploying a system of measurements that both monitors and manages process performance.

TRANSLATING THE MODEL TO ORGANIZATIONAL STRUCTURES

Figure 5.2 illustrates how the previously described roles may be structured. The process council includes and integrates both the functional and process management roles of the enterprise. The council is not necessarily positioned as a separate entity. In fact, it may simply become an extension of the existing management team where process ownership roles are assimilated by existing senior managers (that is, senior managers wear two hats). The process management team (PMT) is a standing cross-functional team that supports an end-to-end business process. The PMT includes representation from each functional unit that participates in the business process. PMT team members play a dual role. They represent the interest of the process to their functional units and they represent the interest of the functional units to the process. Process work is still performed within functional units, although individual jobs are aligned to the processes they support, instead of the functions where they reside. Functional managers focus more on managing the process resources than on managing the performance of work tasks.

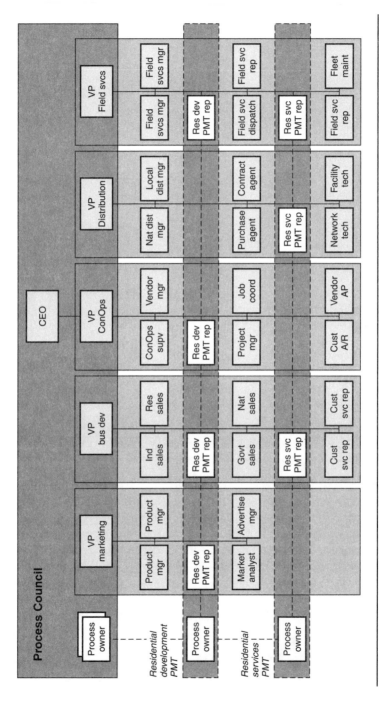

Figure 5.2 PFO enabling structures.

6

Introducing the Process Improvement Road Map

The *Process Improvement Road Map* is offered as a simple mechanism for guiding process improvement and process management work (see Figure 6.1). The road map establishes an order to conducting process work. This ensures that improvement efforts are properly sequenced and that the right tools are utilized.

The road map is based on the concept of process maturity. Six levels of maturity are used to establish a framework for reflecting: (1) the level of understanding associated with a process, (2) the process management practices utilized (for example, standardization, measurement, corrective action, and training), and (3) the resulting performance outcomes (for example, customer satisfaction, process capabilities, competencies, and efficiency). As processes advance along the maturity continuum, they demonstrate higher levels of effectiveness and efficiency. The maturity concept provides a useful framework for guiding process improvement work because: (1) it provides the basis for comparing processes, (2) it recognizes the progression of characteristics needed to build good processes, and (3) it recognizes the need to apply different improvement strategies as processes gain increased maturity.

The road map describes a five-step pathway for systematically advancing business processes along the maturity continuum. Each step builds on the work of the previous steps to apply improvement strategies that are appropriate to the current maturity level. The road map is also designed to respond to the need for near-term improvement results while preserving a long-term focus on developing and sustaining process capability.

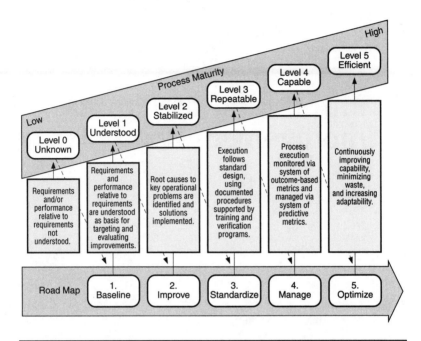

Figure 6.1   The Process Improvement Road Map for systematically advancing process maturity.

This approach builds on two important lessons about planning and conducting process improvement work. First, improvements should focus on advancing the maturity of our processes. The fundamental reality operating here is that seeking improvements at higher levels without first establishing the lower level foundations will not be successful or sustainable. For example, targeting an initiative at improving the capability of a process (a level 4 characteristic) that is not repeatable (a level 3 characteristic) will probably fail. This is a frequent problem when organizations target quick hits early in the implementation cycle. The second lesson is that improvement work must be designed to reflect the types and degree of improvement sought. Here, we're talking about both the approaches used and the time frames allowed for improvement projects. If, for example, we're seeking to jump from level 1 (Understood) to level 4 (Capable), we need to design our project plan and schedule to reflect the complexity of the undertaking. Failing to plan projects without regard to the complexity of the challenge being addressed will yield overruns and poor results.

Process Improvement Reference Guide

The process improvement reference guide (see Figure 6.2) connects improvement strategies with process maturity levels. As the figure illustrates, the transition from each level requires the application of strategies and techniques that are fairly unique to that level.

It is significant to note that the strategies required to advance process maturity are broader than what is prescribed by the Six Sigma or lean methodologies. Consider the baseline step. To establish a complete picture of a process, we should want to know something about the effectiveness of its outcomes, the efficiency and manageability of its operations, and the robustness of its design. Following Six Sigma methods will focus us toward customer-perceived quality, but not toward operational efficiency, while following lean methods will point us toward efficiency, but not to quality. The road map considers all three dimensions of performance.

If processes are indeed key enterprise assets, it stands to reason that we should want those assets to operate at high levels of maturity (that is, repeatable, capable, and so on). However, there is little in the contemporary tool sets that guides us toward developing the standards, supporting infrastructures, control systems, or management practices required to attain and sustain higher levels of performance. The road map and reference guide are designed to fill those gaps via the standardize and manage steps.

The road map is also different from contemporary process improvement methods in other important ways:

1. The road map focuses on improving and managing the capability of end-to-end business processes, not component work process. As we have discussed, improving component subsystems does not necessarily improve the broader system of performance (that is, business process).

2. With the exception of step 2, Improve, the road map is not issue based. Issue-based improvement work responds to specific performance issues that are raised by various stakeholders. The underlying assumption of issue-based work is that if we effectively respond to all of the issues, we will have attained success. It is unlikely, however, that issues will ever focus our attention on the higher levels of capability. I have yet to see an effective system of business process management evolve from an issue-based program.

3. The road map provides a pathway with clearly discernable steps. In my experience using the road map, this is probably the characteristic that is most highly valued by business managers. Unlike issue-based improvement work, the road map provides a clear indication of where you are and what's ahead.

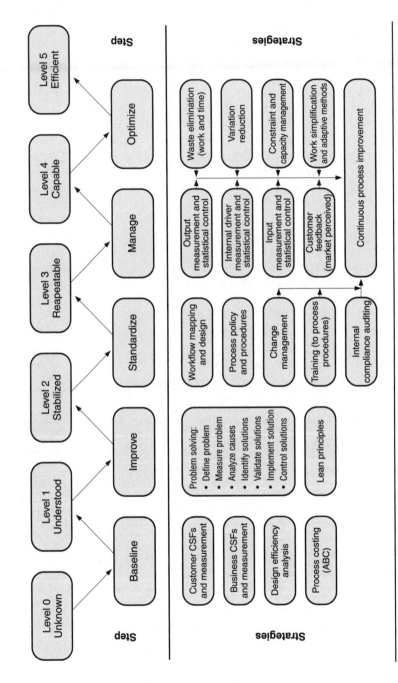

Figure 6.2   The process improvement reference guide.

The following comments provide additional clarification for each road map step.

ROAD MAP STEP 1, BASELINE

The baseline step begins with a process of unknown maturity. The primary objective of this step is to develop a concise understanding of process requirements and performance relative to those requirements. The key outcomes include performance baselines to which future performance improvements can be compared and a gap analysis that indicates performance issues that require resolution. These issues will drive step 2, Improve. The tools and techniques used here include macromapping, customer requirements analysis, business requirements analysis, goal setting, value stream mapping, and analysis and activity-based costing. Completion of the baseline step yields a level 1 (Understood) process. We will discuss the baseline step in greater detail in chapter 9.

Characteristics of a baselined process:

- Customers and requirements are defined and performance relative to requirements is known.

- Business requirements are defined and performance relative to requirements is known.

- Results are unmanaged.

ROAD MAP STEP 2, IMPROVE

The primary objectives of this step are to resolve the key performance gaps identified in the baseline step and to create a stable process environment to enable step 3 work. In step 2 we conduct improvement projects that resolve targeted performance issues. These projects use structured methods that are tailored to the unique needs of each targeted issue. The results of our improvement efforts should be assessed relative to the performance requirements and baselines that were identified in the baseline step. We should stay in step 2 until we have resolved the immediate performance issues for the process. Completion of the improve step yields a level 2, Stabilized, process.

Earlier we mentioned that competency in process improvement must be grown organically. Therefore, we may want to limit step 2 work to relatively simple performance issues so participants can hone their skills. Step 2 is also the ideal time for introducing structured problem solving methods to the organization. Chapter 10 describes the steps for conducting process improvement work in greater detail.

Characteristics of an improved process:

- Key performance deficiencies have been identified and resolved.

- Results are unmanaged (although step 2 improvements should be controlled).

ROAD MAP STEP 3, STANDARDIZE

The primary objective of the standardize step is to create the conditions required to enable consistent execution of the overall process. This is accomplished by establishing and deploying documented policies and procedures to guide process work, training programs to instruct personnel in procedures and skills development, and audit programs to ensure compliance with standards. When step 3 is complete, process execution follows a documented standard process that is enabled by training and verified by a system of auditing. The resulting maturity level, Repeatable, indicates that the process is followed consistently. It does not indicate that the process is deemed repeatable in statistical terms (as in statistical process control). Chapter 11 describes the steps for conducting process standardization work.

Characteristics of a standardized process:

- Work methods are standardized via documented procedures (reflecting appropriate levels of detail).

- The knowledge and ability to perform procedures is assured through a system of training.

- Compliance to procedures is assured via system of auditing.

- A corrective action system is in place to address execution and performance issues.

- Results are managed through postprocess inspection.

ROAD MAP STEP 4, MANAGE

Whereas the previous steps focused on process improvement, step 4 focuses on process management. Here we use the requirements information that was collected in step 1 to establish a system of process performance measurements. These measurements tell us how the process is performing relative to established requirements. Next, we identify the internal determinants of critical process outcomes. By measuring and managing these determinants we are able to proactively manage process performance. Chapter 12 describes the steps to implementing process management methods.

Characteristics of a managed process:

- Customer requirements are translated into output effectiveness measures.

- Output effectiveness measures indicate a repeatable and capable process design.

- Internal effectiveness and efficiency measurements are installed and indicate repeatability.

- There is a favorable trending of customer satisfaction.

ROAD MAP STEP 5, OPTIMIZE

Step 5 is the continuous improvement step. At minimum, optimization work is performed in response to process management results and changing requirements. However, the ultimate goal is to attain a self-sustaining state where continuous improvement is part of the operating culture. Achieving this goal requires that we address two separate elements of organizational design (refer to Figure 3.1 in chapter 3 for an overview of organizational design elements).

The process management system established in step 4 tells us how our process is performing relative to requirements. When these results become unfavorable, process improvement projects are launched to resolve the identified issues. Likewise, when customer or business requirements change, we use improvement projects to develop the capabilities required to fulfill the requirements. The organizational systems element pushes the need for improvement to the organization.

The optimization step also seeks to promote a culture of continuous improvement where improvement work is viewed as a natural and necessary component of organizational life. Here, the organizational culture element actually pulls improvement work from the organization. Establishing the conditions necessary to promote and sustain employee pull requires that we address the sociotechnical elements of organizational life.

As shown in Figure 6.2, the optimize step also introduces more sophisticated techniques to enable our efforts to continuously improve process performance. Chapter 14 describes the steps for conducting process optimization work.

Characteristics of an optimized process:

- Non-value-adding work has been identified and minimized.

- Workflow constraints are identified and managed.

- Internal effectiveness and efficiency measurements are installed and indicate capability.

- Reliance on postprocess inspection is diminishing.

- Internally and externally focused indicators are continuously improving.

Part III

A Transformation Strategy

Part III describes a transformation strategy for guiding the journey to becoming a process-focused organization. The strategy is composed of nine phases that are organized along three tracks (see Figure III.1). The strategy is designed to be executed in phase sequence, with phases 1 through 6 positioned as start-up activities and phases 7 through 9 positioned as ongoing activities.

The program management track includes the activities and responsibilities required to plan, launch, and sustain the program management component of the operating model. This track is performed at the enterprise level by senior managers to provide overall leadership and direction for the program. The track includes two start-up phases and one ongoing phase. The start-up phases focus on understanding value and value streams, identifying and grading enterprise processes, setting process goals, and initiating process management infrastructures. The ongoing phase includes the activities required to oversee priority processes, maintain organizational alignment, leverage process improvements, and maintain process performance and improvement goals.

The process management track includes the activities and responsibilities required to systematically move the process along the Process Improvement Road Map. Phase 3, Understand and Baseline Process, baselines process performance and identifies initial improvement needs. Phase 5, Standardize Process, establishes a repeatable process along with the appropriate supporting infrastructures. Phase 6, Institute Process Management, creates a performance management system to both monitor and

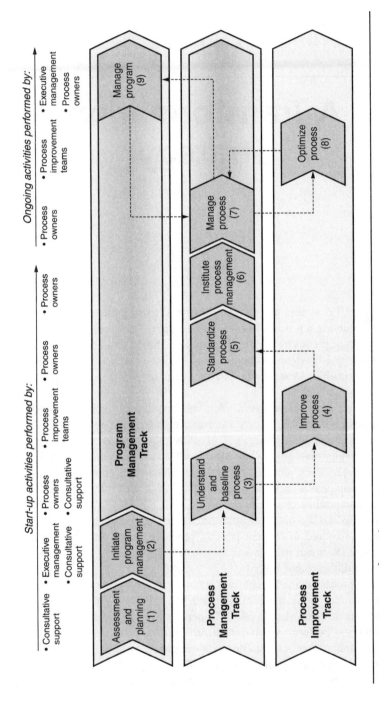

Figure III.1 PFO transformation strategy.

manage process outcomes. The track concludes with phase 7, which includes the activities required to sustain process management and to drive continuous improvement.

The process improvement track is the engine of process improvement. Phase 4 conducts process improvement projects to address the performance issues that were surfaced in phase 3 (Baseline), while phase 9 is positioned as the continuous improvement phase where we seek to attain a self-sustaining culture of improvement.

The remaining chapters of this book describe the implementation strategy in greater detail. In some instances, specific approaches or tools will be offered as suggestions (for example, job descriptions and prioritization techniques). These approaches may be tailored as appropriate to fit preferences or circumstances. Since this operating model is a highly interdependent system, however, the overall architecture of the system should be preserved and each of the five system components should be fully implemented.

7
Phase 1, Assessment and Planning

Process focus must be positioned as a means to improve business outcomes, not as an end in itself. Therefore, it is important that we convert the intellectual arguments covered in the previous chapters into terms that are relevant to our management before engaging them. Trying to sell process principles without first establishing clear linkages to relevant business outcomes can be a serious tactical error. Phase 1 seeks to establish these linkages.

In phase 1 we conduct the analysis required to build the business case for process focus and to gain the requisite support for implementation. It may be a good idea to consider using consultative support to perform this work since it involves skills and resources that may not be readily available. It is also important to perform this work carefully and completely since it will have a large impact on the success of phase 2 (where your management becomes involved).

Figure 7.1 provides a high-level view of the activities that comprise phase 1.

1.1 UNDERSTAND VALUE

As we've said before, the mission of business is to create and deliver value to customers. Value creation is why organizations exist and is what ultimately determines their success in the marketplace. Value is a customer-centric concept that is meaningful only when defined in terms of specific products and/or services. Since these products and services are created by processes, value delivery is process-determined.

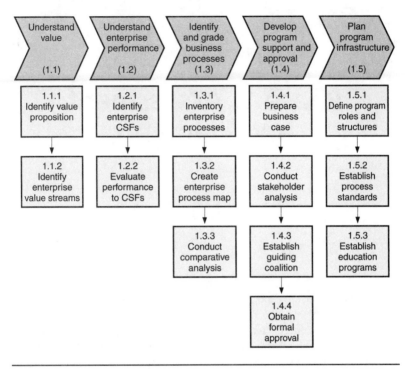

Figure 7.1   The activities of phase 1, Assessment and Planning.

1.1.1 Identify Enterprise Value Proposition

The place to begin is by understanding the value proposition of your organization. The value proposition describes the benefits and pricing arrangements of your products and services that attract customers and that support enterprise financial goals. In short, the value proposition describes why customers buy from you, instead of from your competitors.

It is important to gain a clear understanding of your value proposition very early since it provides the foundation for most of what follows—including identifying value-creating processes, evaluating the value contribution of work, and aligning internal structures, systems, and measurements.

1.1.2 Identify Enterprise Value Creation Streams

Identifying the enterprise value creation streams helps us understand how value is created and delivered to the marketplace. A value creation stream is comprised of the key activities that are required to take a product or service from initial concept to the hands of the end customer (see Figure 7.2).

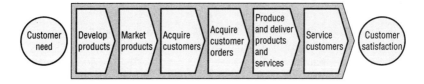

Figure 7.2   Value creation stream.

Tracing the flow of value creation through the enterprise will help us identify our value-creating business processes later.

1.2 UNDERSTAND ENTERPRISE PERFORMANCE

The next step in our assessment work is to develop a clear understanding of how enterprise performance is judged, the key performance issues that are nagging management, and the strategies and action plans that are being executed to resolve those performance issues. It's important to focus on enterprise-level performance right now, so this is not the time to get bogged down in operational minutiae.

1.2.1 Identify Enterprise Critical Success Factors

First identify how enterprise performance is judged. This information can be obtained from a variety of sources, including strategic planning documents, annual reports, performance measurements, customer and employee feedback, and interviews with senior managers. As you collect information, be sure to avoid defining performance too narrowly. Instead, try to develop a broad and balanced perspective. The following dimensions describe a balanced framework for describing organizational performance that borrows from Kaplan and Norton's Balanced Scorecard.[1] Like the Kaplan and Norton approach, the first two dimensions relate to outcomes, while the second two describe drivers of outcome:

    a. *Customer perspective.* Identify the conditions that indicate positive customer-related outcomes. Examples might include high levels of customer retention, improving repurchase behaviors, and customer referrals.

    b. *Financial perspective.* Identify the conditions that indicate satisfactory financial outcomes. Examples might include return on assets, profitable product and service lines, growing market share, and new market penetration.

    c. *Internal capability perspective.* Identify the capabilities and competencies the organization must excel at. Examples might include high levels of quality and operational efficiency, results that are right the first time, little waste or rework, and high skill levels.

    d. *Strategy perspective.* Identify the things the organization must do today to meet future needs. What are the strategies and the approaches to deploying them? How do you know the strategies are being effectively deployed and that they are producing the desired outcomes?

The outcome of this research should be a set of critical success factors (CSFs) that are used by senior management to evaluate and manage enterprise performance. Understanding these factors early is important for two reasons: (1) they provide the context for communicating the value of process to leaders in terms that are relevant to them, and (2) they provide the focus and constancy required to prioritize and align your efforts going forward. Proceeding without a clear understanding of these performance factors is risky, so be sure to devote the time and energy required to accurately understand and validate them before continuing.

1.2.2 Evaluate Performance Relative to CSFs

Now that we know how performance is judged, the question is, how well are we performing? We answer this question by researching each CSF to gain insight into current performance practices and results.

First, we want to learn more about our performance relative to the customer-focused CSFs and about the nature of key customer issues concerning the products and services they are receiving. Usually, this information can be obtained from existing information sources such as satisfaction surveys, complaints, and marketing studies. Another good source of information is your customer contact personnel. As we identify customer-focused information, it is important that we identify the specific products and service dimensions involved. This helps identify the specific processes that are driving these issues.

Next, we want to learn more about the performance of the financially focused CSFs. Although this is the category that generally has the most information available, it is highly likely this information provides little insight into the cost of the business processes. Depending on time and resources, you may want to consider conducting an ABC assessment to develop estimates of process- and product-related costs. This information can be invaluable in supporting our business case since it shines light on areas that were previously unseen. ABC-based assessments can be conducted fairly quickly when used as a high-level estimation tool. The principles underlying ABC are straightforward (that is, products and services are produced via work activities, these activities consume resources and resource consumption incurs costs). Additional information regarding ABC methods is included in step 3.5 in phase 3, Analyze Process Costs.

The internal capabilities category includes the CSFs that focus on internal capabilities and competencies. Performance information relative to this category of CSFs is probably not readily available, so we probably need to survey key business stakeholders.

Strategy includes the CSFs that focus on how the enterprise plans for the future (primarily strategy development and deployment). The easiest way to collect this information is to survey key business stakeholders.

Expect to spend most of your time researching customer and financial performance. Since financial performance will probably end up having the greatest impact on your business case, it is the area we want to understand most thoroughly at this stage. Conducting the ABC assessment now might slow you down on the front end, but can pay ample dividends later.

1.3 IDENTIFY AND GRADE BUSINESS PROCESSES

While it's reasonable to say that business results are largely determined by business processes, it's not reasonable to say that all processes contribute equally to business performance. It's important, therefore, to focus our efforts in the areas that provide the greatest leverage.

We use the concept of priority processes to help ensure that we focus our efforts in the right areas. Priority processes are those processes that are: (1) essential to enterprise success and (2) are not meeting performance expectations. The rationale is that greater results can be obtained by managing and improving important processes than by pursuing improvements to unimportant processes.

The steps that follow are designed to help identify and grade business processes. We do this by identifying business processes, establishing the criteria we will use to grade them, and conducting a comparative assessment. The assessment will identify the processes that require immediate attention.

1.3.1 Inventory Enterprise Processes

The first step is to inventory the business, management, and support processes operating within the enterprise. It's important to remember that we're seeking to identify the big processes that comprise the enterprise. While there may be hundreds of work processes in an organization, there are far fewer business, management, and support processes (commonly around 25 or so). Figure 3.3 in chapter 3 provides examples of the processes that occupy these three categories. While the management and support processes tend to be fairly standardized, business processes tend to more uniquely reflect the value creation streams of enterprises. Therefore, we will devote most of our attention to identifying the business processes.

One approach to recognizing business processes begins by tracing the key transformational states that occur along the flow of value creation. Figure 7.3 provides an example of the key transformational states (or outcomes) that reside along the value stream for an outsourcing enterprise. As shown in the figure, each state change can be associated with the business processes that produce the change. The key to making this approach work is in identifying a small number of relevant states that describe the flow of value creation.

Another approach to identifying business processes is to identify the key customer contact points. These contact points (sometimes referred to as *moments of truth*) are the key leverage points for fueling customer loyalty or dissatisfaction. Developing a customer lifecycle diagram helps identify the contact points and impacted customers.

After we've identified our value-creating business processes, the next step is to identify the processes that support the value-creating processes. Support processes are the class of processes that are essential to enabling the successful operation of our value-creating processes. Examples of support processes might include marketing research, qualifying customers, managing inventory, managing projects, acquiring personnel, training personnel resources, and so on. Some support processes are unique to enterprise while others may be fairly standardized across enterprises. For example, a manufacturing enterprise may utilize support processes related to managing inventory or maintaining production equipment, while a software enterprise may utilize support processes related to managing projects or maintaining testing environments. Both organizations, however, would use support processes related to acquiring personnel, paying personnel, or managing financial records. This class of support processes tends to reside in staff or support functions (for example, personnel, facilities, accounting) and is a frequent candidate for outsourcing.

1.3.2 Create an Enterprise Process Map

The *enterprise process map* provides a high-level systems view of the processes and process interdependencies that comprise the enterprise.

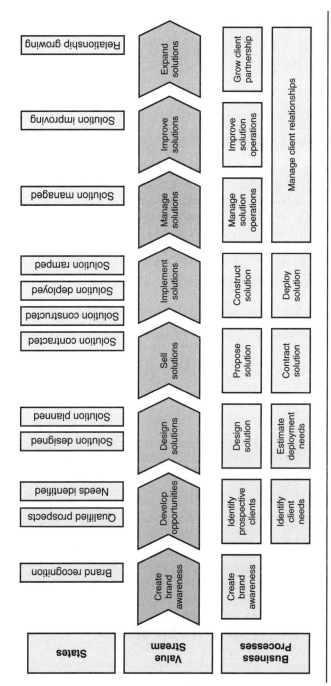

Figure 7.3　Identifying enterprise value stream.

Figure 7.4 provides an example of an enterprise process map for a public utility company. Notice that customer-facing processes are positioned in the upper regions of the map, while background support processes are positioned toward the bottom. Also, the position of each process relative to the value creation stream is indicated via the legend in the lower right corner of the map.

1.3.3 Perform a Comparative Analysis of Processes

Now that we've identified our business and support processes, the question becomes, what is our strategy for dealing with them? In this step we conduct a comparative analysis of our business and support processes to help set our process strategy. The approach described uses a simple two-dimensional scheme that compares process relevance and health. Using this approach, each business and support process is scored in terms of its relevance to value creation and its health relative to performance outcomes. The results of the process-level scoring work are then posted on a two-dimensional grid like that shown in Figure 7.5. Each of the quadrants in the grid points to a potential process strategy for our business and support processes.

Quadrant	Relevance	Health	Process Strategy
Q1	High	Low	Priority process requiring immediate improvement
Q2	High	High	Core competency (a marketplace differentiator to be exploited)
Q3	Low	High	Potential service offering
Q4	Low	Low	Potential outsourcing candidate

Using the data, we can conduct the process assessment exercise. To begin, we establish analysis criteria. The criteria used to describe process relevance might include: (1) the relative importance to attaining enterprise CSFs, (2) the relationship to strategic goals or imperatives, (3) the number of customer contact points (moments of truth), and (4) the proximity to the value creation stream. For each criterion selected, we can establish a grading scale to describe the various intervals of relevance that may be appropriate. Although we're not necessarily striving for numerical precision, we are striving for repeatable measures. Therefore, each interval should be defined using clearly defined outcomes or behaviors. For example, when developing the scale for relative importance to attaining business CSFs, the intervals may be defined as: 5 = absolutely essential to five or more CSFs,

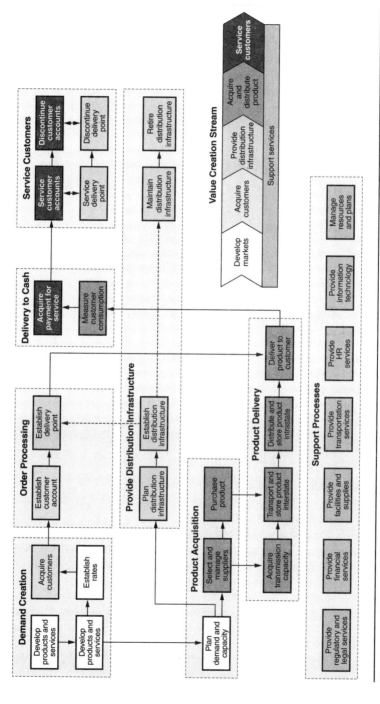

Figure 7.4   The macro enterprise process map.

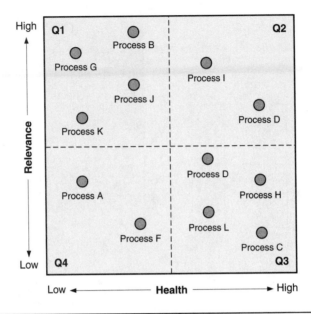

Figure 7.5   Comparing process relevance and health.

4 = absolutely essential to three or more CSFs, 3 = absolutely essential to one CSF, and continuing down to 0 as not essential to any CSFs. When using multiple characteristics to describe relevance, we want to design our measurement scales to enable cross multiplication of the characteristics to produce a combined axis score. For example, if we use the four character- istics just listed to measure relevance, each characteristic may be designed to use a 1 to 5 scale, with 1 being least relevant and 5 being most relevant. Cross multiplying the results of the four characteristics yields a result for the relevance scale. The maximum score using this approach would be 625 and the minimum score would be 1.

Process health can be assessed in terms of (1) how effectively it ful- fills its purpose, (2) how efficiently it fulfills its purpose, and (3) how adaptable it is. Measurement scales can be developed using the same approach discussed for the relevance axis.

When the criteria have been defined and their grading scales estab- lished, the next step is to poll executive and operational mangers to grade the processes. While this is admittedly a simplistic approach to grading processes, it is sufficient to narrow our focus to the processes offering the greatest leverage for improvement results. Moreover, the simplicity of the approach makes it very easy to explain and easy to conduct.

1.4 DEVELOP SUPPORT AND APPROVAL

1.4.1 Prepare the Business Case

We're now ready to prepare a business case that reflects the factors and issues that are relevant to our enterprise managers. While part of the argument for process focus is conceptual, conceptual arguments won't carry the day. So, try to identify examples of performance issues in your organization that are driven by functional structures, improper organizational alignment, disconnected cross-functional processes, and the like. Be sure to include the results of the process assessment work as the basis for suggesting the process areas requiring early attention. Also, consider contrasting your organization's performance with others that are doing it better.

1.4.2 Conduct Stakeholder Analysis

The journey to process focus involves significant organizational change, and change will rouse both supporters and detractors. Supporters with strong influence (either positional or personal) can be key allies to promoting the initiative. Influential detractors, on the other hand, warrant a mitigation strategy.

Stakeholder analysis provides us with a useful tool for identifying, grading, and developing strategies around both groups. Figure 7.6 illustrates the results of a stakeholder analysis exercise. People with large negative impact scores represent the greatest threat to the initiative and require a proactive

Name	Support (–5 to +5)	Influence (1 to 5)	Impact Score (S × I)	Mitigation/Utilization Strategy
R. Gardner	+4	3	9	+ Network with Cohen
J. Bohannan	–3	4	–12	– Principles workshop – Network with Brown, Hoell
D. Greulich	+3	1	3	
J. Brown	+4	4	16	+ Network with Bohannan + Presentations
H. Hatcher	–2	2	–4	– Principles workshop
E. Hoell	+4	3	12	+ Network with Bohannan + Publish to newsletter
H. Cohen	–4	2	–8	– Training – Network with Gardner

Figure 7.6   A sample stakeholder analysis.

mitigation strategy, while people with large positive scores are your potential allies.

The first step is to identify the stakeholders who will influence the decision to launch the PFO initiative as well as the ultimate success of the initiative if adopted. The second step is to gauge their support for the initiative. This information can be obtained via networking and collaborative activities.

1.4.3 Establish a Guiding Coalition

Successful organizational change requires a strong guiding coalition to provide thought leadership, strategy development, and championing of the cause. The coalition should include people who are influential and intellectually and emotionally invested in the change effort. This may or may not include senior management. If senior management is not included in this category, the coalition has the additional role of influencing noninvested managers. The stakeholder analysis helps you identify your supporters.

The guiding coalition does not have to be a formally organized group. It may simply be comprised of an informal network that involves key supporters in determining change strategies, communicating and debating ideas, or lobbying. Regardless of the approach used, it is important to establish ways to leverage supporters.

1.4.4 Obtain Formal Approval

With the help of your guiding coalition, it's now time to plan and present the business case for process focus to senior management for a formal decision to proceed. The preceding steps focused on developing the information required to prepare an effective business case.

1.5 PREPARE PROGRAM INFRASTRUCTURE

The transition to becoming a PFO will impact existing organizational roles and structures, operating practices, and beliefs. The following steps should be carefully considered before moving on to phase 2.

1.5.1 Define Roles and Structures

As mentioned previously, the PFO introduces new organizational roles and responsibilities that must be carefully considered. The first order of business is to determine how the program management and process ownership roles will be defined and implemented, and how process management will work in concert with process execution. When defining these roles it is essential that we describe who is responsible for (1) setting enterprise and process goals, (2) defining and administering process measurements, and (3) managing and improving process performance. Chapter 5 offered practical advice regarding roles and responsibilities in the PFO.

1.5.2 Establish Process Standards

Successful execution of the transformation strategy also depends on the consistent application of process-related operating practices and standards. Operating practices may include how process ownership is exercised; how process management teams will operate; how performance goals and measurements are established, deployed, and used; and how process improvement initiatives are chartered. Formal process standards are required to ensure effective process documentation and may include operating policies and procedures, performance metrics construction and presentation, audit documentation, and other related templates and tools. We will offer considerable advice regarding the formation of process standards throughout the balance of this book.

1.5.3 Establish and Deploy Education Programs

It should be clear that the PFO is based on a new set of paradigms. The success of our implementation effort will, therefore, be largely determined by the degree to which these paradigms are understood and embraced by leaders and managers. The transition to becoming a PFO is also about change. Leaders must also understand and fulfill the leadership requirements related to enabling the significant organizational changes associated with becoming a PFO.

The following learning topics will facilitate the transition process. Unfortunately, there aren't many training programs available on the market that address these topics, so most of your training will have to be home grown.

1. *Process thinking.* This topic seeks to teach executives, managers, and employees the principles associated with process-focused organizations. Strategy deployment, job design, performance management, and improvement methods all require significant rethinking in the process-focused organization.

2. *Change leadership.* Change leadership teaches and/or reinforces the principles of organizational change, identifies the roles and responsibilities of leaders in the change process, and enrolls them in the process.

3. *Process management systems.* This topic teaches senior managers and process owners the fundamentals of process management, including goal setting, measurement definition and deployment, statistical techniques, and compliance auditing.

4. *Process improvement methods.* There are proven methods for conducting process improvement work. Training programs are available for Six Sigma and lean principles to help prepare employees for conducting process improvement work.

5. *Managing in a process environment.* Managing in a process environment is significantly different from managing in a functional organization. This topic seeks to prepare operating managers for the transition from a functionally managed environment to a process-focused environment.

6. *Enterprise process literacy.* This topic involves an ongoing effort to keep employees informed regarding the roles, designs, and performance levels of enterprise processes.[2]

It is absolutely essential that senior executives and managers understand, embrace, and adopt the principles and practices associated with process management and improvement (topics 1 through 4). Otherwise, they will continue to pull the same levers they've always pulled, and the change program will ultimately fail. These topics should be covered with senior leaders before exiting phase 2.

Process management systems (topic 3) should be introduced to process owners and process management teams during phase 2 and mastered in phase 6. Process improvement methods (topic 4) should be covered as process improvement teams are launched (in phases 4 and 8) and managing in a process environment (topic 5) should be covered as process improvements are deployed in operating units. Topic 6 is positioned as ongoing program to continuously inform and educate employees regarding process standards, performance and improvement results.

1.5.4 Establish Deployment Plan

Before leaving phase 1, it is a good idea to prepare a documented deployment plan. Although the plan may be fairly high-level at this point, it must contain sufficient detail to describe key milestones and dates, budget and staffing requirements, accountabilities, and measures. It is important to enter phase 2 with a clear picture of what's ahead so that you can appropriately inform and prepare the senior management team. Entering phase 2 without a clear picture will do little to instill management's confidence in you or your program.

8

Phase 2, Initiate Program Management

As mentioned previously, the program management component provides leadership and the accountabilities required to guide and sustain the transition to a process-focused organization. The process council is positioned as the primary vehicle for fulfilling these responsibilities. The steps required to initiate program management are outlined in this phase, while the steps required to sustain program management are outlined in phase 9. Figure 8.1 illustrates the key steps and work products comprising this phase.

2.1 ESTABLISH AND TRAIN PROCESS COUNCIL

The process council should be comprised of senior enterprise managers and led by the chief executive. Process owners may sit on the council or they may report to the council.

It is essential that senior managers be personally engaged in providing the leadership and maintaining the accountabilities required to promote the program. *These roles cannot be delegated.* If senior management is not fully and personally engaged, the chances of success are greatly reduced. The good news is that the time involved in these roles is minimal (several hours per month) and can normally be integrated into existing activities.

Initial (one-time) responsibilities for the process council include: (1) determining priority processes, (2) establishing goals for priority processes, and (3) selecting and training process owners and operating managers. These responsibilities are described in this phase (phase 2).

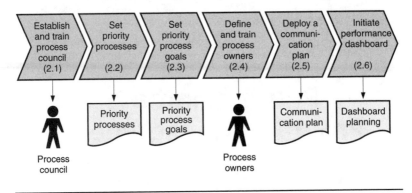

Figure 8.1 The activities of phase 2, Initiate Program Management.

Ongoing responsibilities for the process council include: (1) monitoring priority process performance and interventions, (2) ensuring alignment between priority processes and organizational structures and systems, and (3) leveraging improvements across operating divisions (where appropriate). These responsibilities are outlined in phase 9.

It is important that process council members be well grounded in the principles of process-focused organizations, as well as have a basic understanding of process management and improvement strategies and techniques. It is difficult to effectively lead a change initiative without having clear understanding and alignment around the vision and key ideas involved.

2.2 DETERMINE PRIORITY PROCESSES

In order to resolve focus, the process council may want to select a small number of processes that are designated as *priority processes.* Priority processes are those that are essential to enterprise success (high in relevance) and not meeting performance expectations (low in health). The information collected in phase 1, step 3 was designed to facilitate a criterion-based assessment along these dimensions to help identify your priority processes.

2.3 SET PRIORITY PROCESS PERFORMANCE GOALS

After the priority processes are set, the next step is to translate the enterprise-level CSFs to the priority processes in the form of process goal statements.

Each goal statement should describe a particular process-level outcome (or state) that is necessary to fulfill one or more enterprise CSFs. Combined, these statements comprise the process vision for each priority process. Successful completion of this step requires:

- Establishing consensus regarding the enterprise CSFs, which may simply involve affirming or adjusting the work performed in phase 1, step 2 or may require additional information gathering and analysis.

- Identifying causal linkages between enterprise CSFs and the priority processes—thereby formally recognizing the key interdependencies that exist between the priority business processes and enterprise outcomes.

- Establishing process-level goal statements for CSF–process linkages by describing the process state required to enable successful outcomes.

The overarching purpose of this work is to resolve focus around the process performance dimensions that are important while maintaining clear linkages between those dimensions and enterprise-level results. *The importance of this work cannot be overemphasized because it establishes the foundation for all process improvement and process management work that follows.* While we may be inclined to start investigating what performance measures are available or what characteristics are measurable, that can be a mistake at this point. What is available or measurable may not be what's important to enterprise performance.

To set process goals, express process goals as a *state*. Process goals should describe desired end states for the process. This is accomplished by expressing goals as the conditions (or states) that must exist to satisfy the process vision. For example, an end state goal for a customer field service process might be as simple as "customer-requested appointment times are met." Expressing goals as end states helps us later when we're setting performance targets. This is not the time to make our goals specific, measurable, actionable, reasonable, and timely (SMART). We will operationalize our goals later in the process. At this point, we're simply trying to understand the process states that describe our vision of success.

Balanced process goals should be established to ensure that appropriate emphasis is given to the various and sometimes competing dimensions of performance. For example, emphasizing near-term goals at the expense of long-term goals will generally result in behaviors and decisions that trade long-term capabilities for short-term gains. Or, emphasizing cost goals at the expense of quality goals may degrade quality performance. Balance is necessary to optimize performance.

When setting process goals, consider the dimensions outlined in Figure 8.2. These dimensions borrow from Kaplan and Norton's Balanced Scorecard and translate them to the process level of performance.[1] Like the Balanced Scorecard, the vertical axis focuses on outcomes while the horizontal axis focuses on the determinants of those results. Using this approach helps us in two ways:

1. It promotes a balanced perspective of performance.

2. It provides the foundation for developing a performance management system that proactively influences outcomes by quantitatively managing the determinants of those outcomes.

It's important to set our process goals early and with the right stakeholders in order to establish a solid foundation for subsequent work. We will use the goals established here as the basis for conducting process baseline work in phase 3 and for establishing our process management system in phase 6.

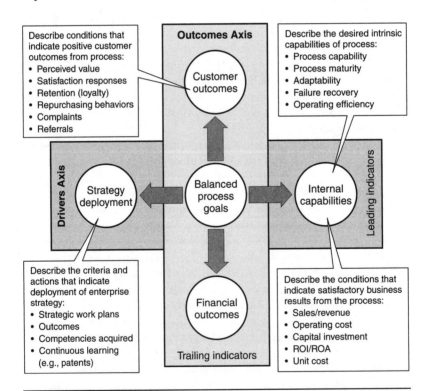

Figure 8.2 Framework for balanced process goals.

2.3.1 Set Customer-Focused Process Goals

Whereas CSFs are the criteria used by enterprise management to evaluate and manage enterprise performance, customer requirements are the criteria customers use to evaluate our performance. Since customers are the final judges of our business processes, it is essential that we understand performance from their perspective.

If there is a formalized mechanism that regularly collects and interprets customer requirements, this information may already be available. If there is no such mechanism, talk with your customers. This information is too important to rely on assumptions or guesswork, so be sure to talk with the process customers, if at all possible. Measuring performance against the wrong requirements may be worse than not measuring at all.

If there is a large number of customers and/or customer types who interact with the process, it may be helpful to establish classification schemes that combine similar customers. These schemes may reflect location on the value stream (for example, distributor or end user), type of customer (for example, commercial, residential, or consumer), geographical characteristics (for example, region or nation), or the customer's intended use of the products or services produced. Process-related requirements may then be identified for each customer classification. Customer-related requirements generally fall into two categories: product-related, where requirements are expressed as product attributes, and service-related, where requirements are expressed behaviorally.

Customer perceptions of performance are largely determined by their perceptions of value. As we discussed earlier, value is an economic concept that considers the benefits obtained from using a product or service as well as the cost of acquiring and using the product or service. This means understanding your customers' perceptions of value is an essential prerequisite to setting customer-related performance goals.

It may be helpful to clarify the difference between customer satisfaction and customer-perceived value. Satisfaction can be described as a response that is related to the degree of alignment that exists between value expectations and perceived value delivered. To the degree there is alignment, customer satisfaction responses tend to be positive. Satisfaction can be measured, but not directly acted upon. Value delivery, on the other hand, can be measured and managed.

When establishing customer performance goals, it is helpful to consider customer contact points and delivered product. Customer contact points are where service occurs. These moments of truth are the primary leverage points for influencing customer satisfaction or dissatisfaction. The key to developing process goals around customer contact points is to identify and understand the transactions that take place during each contact. These transactions can then be decomposed into the customer-desired service behaviors that signal positive outcomes. Note that timeliness and convenience are viewed as service behaviors.

Customers have expectations regarding the products they purchase. These expectations need to be understood and then translated into the product attributes that support them. Product attributes may include physical characteristics, features, reliability, or serviceability.

Remember, at this point we're only trying to identify customer-focused goals. This is not the time to get involved with measurement issues. Don't worry about what data are available or how goals might be measured. That will come later.

2.3.2 Set Business-Focused Process Goals

In addition to providing value to customers, business processes must provide economic gain to the business enterprise. All business enterprises have expectations regarding revenues, costs, margins, return on investment, and the like. Process-level financial goals should be established to reflect direct linkages to the financial metrics used to manage the enterprise and should reflect long-term as well as short-term goals. This work may be accomplished by asking senior enterprise managers how they judge business and financial performance for both the entire enterprise and your business process.

2.3.3 Set Strategy-Related Process Goals

Processes should also be evaluated and managed in terms of their ability to support strategic goals and plans. So be sure to review your enterprise-level strategic goals, measures, and action plans to identify relevant interdependencies between strategy and your priority business processes.

2.3.4 Set Internal Performance Process Goals

This dimension deals with any intrinsic capabilities or characteristics that are desired from our processes.

Efficiency. Efficiency deals with the extent to which resources are minimized and waste eliminated in a process. The resources generally included in this category are people, equipment, and capital. As processes are made more efficient, they are more cost-effective to operate.

Lead Time. Lead time is the time required to complete the end-to-end process. Generally, shorter lead times offer greater responsiveness to customers, enable adaptability to changing requirements, require less working capital, produce less waste, and cause fewer errors. Lead time is determined by size (number of steps) and flow rate (velocity) of a process. The key to impacting flow rates is to know and manage process constraints.

Other. There will most likely be other internal characteristics that determine the success of our processes. Characteristics that might fall into this category include manageability, adaptability, robustness, failure recovery, and learning.

Using the balance approach to setting process goals positions us to understand success (by measuring the characteristics on the outcomes axis) and to proactively manage success (by managing the characteristics on the drivers axis).

2.4 DEFINE, TRAIN, AND CHARTER PROCESS OWNERS

Next, the process council should select process owners for the priority processes, communicate the process level goal statements to the process owners, and ensure the process owners and impacted operating managers are trained in appropriate topics (see phase 1, step 5).

2.5 DEVELOP AND DEPLOY A COMMUNICATION PLAN

Effective communications are needed to ensure organizational awareness regarding the program. These communications should include the reasons for the program, near- and long-term objectives, near- and long-term impacts on the organization, operating plans, and management expectations. The process council should define and execute a communications plan that communicates these points on a regular basis. Council members should personally participate in these communications when and where possible.

2.6 INITIATE ENTERPRISE PERFORMANCE DASHBOARD

Although the measurement vision should ultimately include the full range of cause and effect relationships that drive enterprise performance, the place to begin building your measurement system is with the enterprise-level CSFs. The process council should take responsibility for ensuring the performance dashboard is initiated based on enterprise-level CSFs (including measurement definitions and related targets) and that process-level measurements are subsequently integrated.

9

Phase 3, Baseline Processes

P hase 3 is where we establish the organization and knowledge required to manage and improve processes. It is the first step on the process management track and is performed at the business process level. This is where we develop a clear understanding of key process performance requirements and establish quantified measures of performance relative to those requirements. As shown in Figure 9.1, developing this understanding advances our processes to maturity level one (understood) on the Process Improvement Road Map.

Baselining is an essential first step to process work. Although it takes some time to perform and may seem like a distraction from real process work, baselining ensures that we focus our initial improvement efforts on the right issues as well as provides us with a sound basis for measuring the impact of improvement efforts. The baseline phase sets the stage for the improve phase by systematically identifying the near-term improvement needs for each priority process. Figure 9.2 illustrates the six steps that comprise the baseline phase.

The key role in this work is the process owner. As mentioned previously, the process owner's primary responsibility is to provide the enterprise with a process that is capable of meeting enterprise performance requirements. This means the owner is responsible for the design of the process. In operational terms, process ownership also involves oversight of process documentation and training materials, monitoring the integrity of compliance and the effectiveness of operations, and driving continuous improvement. Although the owner does not manage day-to-day operation of the process

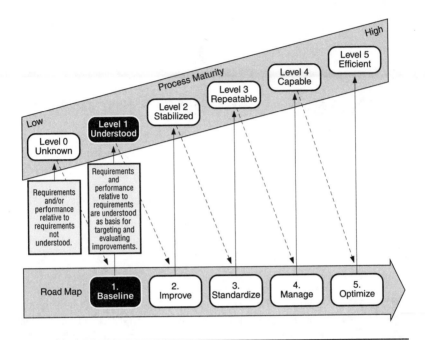

Figure 9.1   The Process Improvement Road Map for systematically advancing process maturity.

(that is still handled by operating managers), it is essential that the owner be informed regarding operational compliance and effectiveness of the process. This information is provided via process metrics and audits.

In phase 3, the process owner and process management team (PMT) conduct a thorough review of the end-to-end process. The objectives of this review include: (1) clarifying process scope, (2) understanding process requirements, (3) understanding performance relative to requirements, (4) understanding operational characteristics, and (5) identifying improvement priorities. The review should not be limited to a review of operational documentation and records. It should also include direct observation and interviews of frontline workers and support personnel to ensure the PMT members learn how the process is *actually* performed, not just how it *should be* performed.

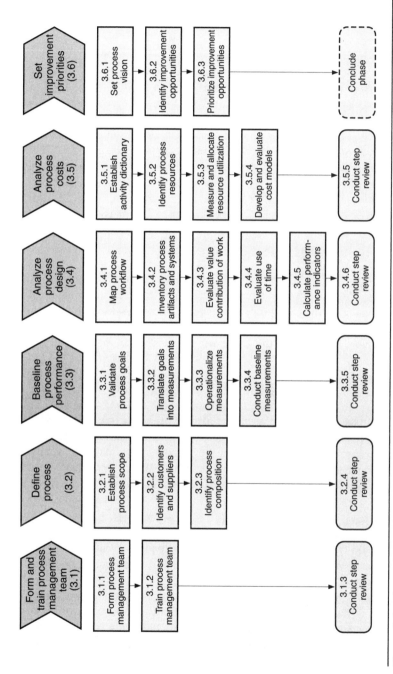

Figure 9.2 The activities of phase 3, Baseline.

3.1 FORM AND TRAIN PROCESS MANAGEMENT TEAM

3.1.1 Form Process Management Team

The first step for the process owner is to form the PMT. The PMT is a standing team that includes representatives from each organizational component (location or department) that participates in the cross-functional process. PMT members serve dual roles. First, they bring the insights and perspectives of their respective organizations to the team, and second, they champion the interests of the process within their organizations. The process owner serves as the team leader. The time commitment for PMT members during the assessment phase may be on the order of 20 percent for several months. Thereafter, it should drop to around five percent.

3.1.2 Train Process Management Team

Members of the PMT must be well grounded in the principles of process-focused organizations and change leadership. They must also begin with a basic understanding of process management and process improvement strategies and techniques. This level of understanding should be expanded as the team moves along the implementation pathway.

3.2 DEFINE PROCESS

The purpose of this step is to ensure that we begin with clear definitions of the process scope, composition, operating environment, and stakeholders. Since we're seeking to understand the process as a whole, the details of internal operations are not relevant right now. This work establishes the foundation for the measurement work that will follow.

3.2.1 Establish Process Scope

We begin by identifying the beginning and ending events that form the boundaries of the process. The beginning events are commonly referred to as entry events and the ending events as exit events (see Figure 9.3). A beginning event is triggered by the receipt of an external input, called a *driver*. Drivers are what cause processes to do work. There can be multiple exit events, with each yielding one or more products or services. The series of linked activities that occur between entry and exit events are part of the process space.

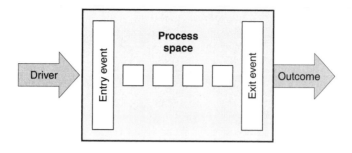

Figure 9.3 Setting process scope.

3.2.2 Identify Process Customers and Suppliers

Customers initiate our business processes. That is to say that customers supply the drivers that cause our processes to do work. Of course, customers also receive the outcomes of our processes in the form of products and services. Customers include the people and organizations who interact with the process or its outcomes, as well as those who make purchasing decisions. The simplest way to identify customers is to examine all of the interactions that occur along the customer lifecycle. These moments of truth represent opportunities to positively or negatively impact value delivery to our customers.

Process suppliers provide the resources required to perform process work. These resources may include the materials, information, or services that are consumed by processes.

3.2.3 Identify Process Composition

It is helpful if we can organize our business process into a small number of key subprocesses. The subprocesses should be defined such that each produces a clearly defined outcome. This helps us assure that subprocess boundaries are distinct, with no overlap. Figure 7.3 provided an example of how process outcomes can be used to identify and name subprocesses.

After we've identified the subprocesses that comprise our priority business process, the next step is to identify the functional units that participate in the process. It is helpful to define the first-level subprocesses such that each functional unit has clear ownership of a single subprocess. Figure 9.4 shows how a cross-functional business process may be decomposed into subprocesses that align with the functional organizations that support the process.

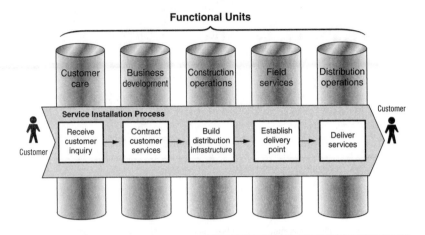

Figure 9.4   Decomposing a business process across organizational functions.

3.3 BASELINE PERFORMANCE

We're now ready to establish our initial measurements of process performance based on the process goals that were set in phase 2. These measurements will help us identify our improvement priorities and evaluate the effects of our improvement work.

3.3.1 Validate Process Goals

Since baseline measurement work will require substantial commitments of time and energy, it's a good idea to validate the process goals with key stakeholders before going forward. In this case, your key stakeholders are customers and senior enterprise managers.

3.3.2 Translate Goals into Measurements

The goal–question–metric (GQM) technique provides us with a straightforward and proven method for developing measurements based on goals. The technique uses the following three-step approach to developing measurements.

1. *Establish process goals.* This work was actually completed in the previous step. It is included here simply to allow us to follow a series of examples through application of the GQM technique.

An example of process goals.

Goal #	Goal Type	Definition
1	Customer	Customer-requested service appointment times are met.

2. *Translate goals into questions.* After process goals are defined, the next step is to determine what questions must be answered to know if the goals are satisfied. It is generally best to develop two or three questions for each goal. The answers to these questions can serve as cross-checks for one another.

An example of translating goals into questions.

Goal #	Goal	Questions
1	Customer-requested appointment times are met.	
1		Are appointments being scheduled as requested by customers?
1		Are scheduled appointments met?

3. *Translate questions into measurements.* After we've identified the questions, the next step is to identify the measurements that are needed to answer the questions.

An example of translating questions into measurements.

Goal	Question	Measurement
Customer-requested appointment times are met.		
	Are appointments being scheduled as requested by customers?	
		Ratio of appointments scheduled as requested to the total number of appointments booked.
	Are scheduled appointments met?	
		Ratio of appointments met to the total number of appointments scheduled.

When developing measurements, try to fulfill the following criteria for good measurements:

- They are sensitive to the right things and insensitive to others.

- They are appropriate for analysis and action.

- They are normalized for comparability between measurement items.

- They can be plotted over time.

- They can be rolled up or summarized meaningfully for higher-level reporting.

- They are easy to understand.

- They are easy to obtain.

The informational value of measurements can be greatly increased when they are normalized. Generally, this involves expressing them as ratios or multiples.

Here's an example of measurement normalization. Customers of a service organization were complaining that service representatives were missing scheduled appointments. Initial efforts that simply tracked the number of appointments missed per month were found to be misleading when it was realized that the measurement could indicate worsened performance when performance actually improved (for example, when missed appointments increase at a rate that is slower than total appointments). This was resolved by normalizing the measure to indicate the number of appointments missed per hundred appointments scheduled. This new measure better describes the performance being measured and is comparable across measurement items.

3.3.3 Operationalize Measurements

Now that we've determined what we need to measure, the next step is to convert our measurement concepts into terms that are actionable. This involves determining the specific data elements we must record to drive our measurements, establishing the operational definitions required to enable collection and storage of these data elements, and determining the analysis categories and targets that will be used to analyze our data.

a. *Identify measurement data elements.* Frequently, process measurements are actually comprised of several lower order data elements. For example, the measurement "ratio of appointments scheduled as requested to the total number of appointments booked" is comprised of two data elements (the number of appointments scheduled as requested and the number of appointments booked). While measurements are what get reported and analyzed, data elements are what actually get recorded and tracked. Measurements may only exist in a data dictionary, while data elements reside in our databases and files. It is helpful to view data elements as the raw materials from which measurements are formed.

b. *Operationalize measurements and data elements.* Even though you may feel your measurement definitions are fairly specific at this point, it is likely that you will need to define additional details regarding both the measurements and their component data elements. These details are essential to ensuring clarity and to flushing out technical challenges related to establishing, collecting, managing, and analyzing your measurements. Poorly defined measures are potentially troublesome measures. Consider the following when refining measurements and data element definitions:

- *Operational definition.* Describing measurement elements in precise, unambiguous terms.

- *Data type.* Describing the format and intervals associated with the data element.

- *Data sources.* Describing where the data will come from (that is, systems or data collection activities).

- *Data population.* Describing what is included and/or excluded from the measurement item.

- *Sampling approach.* Describing sampling methods, if used.

- *Recording frequency.* Describing how frequently measurements will be taken.

c. *Set analysis categories and targets.* It may be helpful to develop classification schemes that divide our measurement data into relevant subgroups. The use of subgroups facilitates sensitivity to subgroup differences and increases the effectiveness of subsequent data analysis. For example, the order entry rates for different classes of customers or products may have characteristics that are sufficiently different to warrant stratification and analysis at the customer class level.

We may also want to establish target values for the measurement population or subgroups to enable exception or codified reporting later in the manage process phase. In exception reporting, results data are not reported unless they exceed preestablished targets. In codified reporting, performance results may be coded (for example, green, yellow, or red) based on their proximity to the target value. Measurement dashboards frequently use codified reporting.

3.3.4 Conduct Baseline Measurements

It's now time to establish the initial readings for our process measurements. In some cases the required information and data may be readily available, while in other cases, we may be faced with collecting information from scratch. Although the preferred method for collecting performance data is via direct measurement, we may be constrained in terms of time and resources. Sampling and estimation are appropriate tools for developing baseline measurements.

This is not the time to get mired in extensive studies. Since our primary goal is to quickly estimate performance to help with targeting improvements, measurement precision is not critical at this time. It is important, however, that our measurement techniques be repeatable so they can be used later in the improve process phase to detect improvements in process performance.

3.4 ANALYZE PROCESS DESIGN

3.4.1 Map Process Workflow

The easiest way to understand how a process works is to walk through it from beginning to end. Generally, this involves a combination of interviewing and observation. Although you may begin your interviews with management personnel, it is best to rely on frontline personnel for the real facts. At this stage, observation should be reserved for areas that can not be understood through interviews.

It is a good idea to document your process using a process map. The map provides a baseline representation of the process and enables team members to develop a common understanding of the process. It is also a good idea to validate your map with process performers to ensure you accurately recorded how the process operates. The brown paper mapping technique provides a simple and effective approach to mapping at this stage.

The level of detail depends on the types of analysis you plan to conduct. Since we plan to evaluate the value contribution of work, the use of time, and process costs, we should map at the who-does-what level of detail. At this level of detail, whenever the performer, work object, or transforming activity changes, we want to record a step on our workflow map.

3.4.2 Inventory Process Artifacts and Systems

Although technology and information systems may be key determinants of process capability, they are rarely identified as explicit process elements. Process documentation and supporting artifacts are frequently not cataloged as well. If you do not have an accurate inventory of these components, it is a fairly simple matter to record this information as you map the process.

3.4.3 Evaluate Value Contribution of Work

The process workflow map identifies the work that is required to execute the process. Not all of this work is equally relevant to the creation of value, however. In order to gain insight into the relevance of the work contained in our process, our next step is to categorize each of the work steps identified in our workflow map as one of the following:

Value adding (VA). This is work that creates customer-perceived value. It is work that: (1) changes the state or form of the work object, (2) in a way the customer wants, and (3) is the first time performed.

Value enabling (VE). This is work that creates no value, but is required to enable the process. Removal of this work will cause the process to fail, so it must be designed out.

Waste work (WW). This is work that neither adds nor enables value. Since waste work is not required to enable process operation, it can be removed without requiring redesign. Examples include rechecking, following up, and rework.

The results of this analysis can be recorded directly on the workflow map. I usually record the value classification code (*VA, VE,* or *WW*) in the lower left-hand portion of each process step.

3.4.4 Evaluate Use of Time

In this step we measure process time and lead time. We estimate the process time to produce a single unit of process output by determining the time required to complete each of the individual work steps that comprise our process. The aggregated process time represents the amount of work that must be invested to produce a unit of output. We can measure the process times for each step or we can estimate them. I prefer to estimate step-level process times by asking the people who perform the work to estimate a time range and an associated probability for each value. For example, an employee may estimate the time to complete a step as ranging from 10 to 20 minutes, where 10 minutes is required for easy orders and 20 minutes is required for difficult orders. Next, the employee may estimate that approximately 70 percent of the orders are easy orders. From these data, we can establish a single point estimate of 13 minutes. While the approach is not precise, it is better than simply asking for a point estimate.

We estimate the lead time to produce a single unit of output by measuring the beginning and ending clock times and calculating the difference.

The difference between the lead time and the total process time gives us an estimate of the idle time present in the process.

3.4.5 Calculate Process Performance Ratios

We can use the data generated in steps 3.4.3 and 3.4.4 to calculate the following process ratios:

Process efficiency, which is the percentage of lead time that is value-adding process time

Time utilization, which is the percentage of lead time that is consumed by work

Work utilization, which is the percentage of process time that is value-adding work

The process efficiency ratio provides insight into the degree of leanness associated with a process. A process with an efficiency ratio greater than 25 percent is generally considered a world-class lean process.[1] The time utilization ratio provides a snapshot of how effectively a process uses time. Low time utilization ratios generally indicate greater opportunity to compress lead time by reducing internal idle time by application of lean techniques. And finally, the work utilization ratio provides a snapshot of how effectively the process utilizes resources in the performance of work. The lower the work utilization ratio, the greater the degree of resource waste operating in a process. Lean techniques also help us reduce resource waste.

3.5 ANALYZE PROCESS COSTS

Traditional accounting methods generally provide little insight regarding the true costs associated with operating an end-to-end business process. If cost is an important consideration to your management, consider using an ABC process improvement diagnostic to estimate and evaluate process costs. Much of the work required to conduct this analysis has already been completed, so the challenge isn't as great as one might fear. The information generated by this technique can be invaluable to baselining cost performance and identifying cost-related improvement needs.

The logic underlying ABC is straightforward—first, products and services are produced by activities; second, activities consume enterprise resources; and third, resource consumption incurs cost. By enabling us to develop cost estimates of activities, ABC supports the two cost views described in Figure 9.5. When activities are aggregated by product, we have

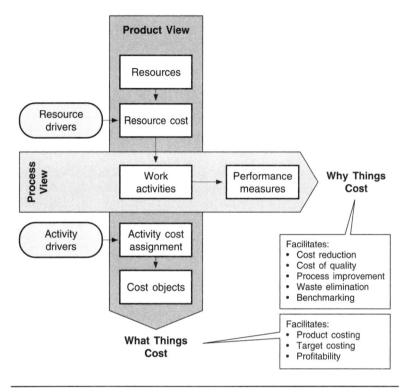

Figure 9.5 Multiple cost views of ABC.

insight into the costs associated with producing the product. When activities are aggregated by process, we have insight into the cost composition of process work.

Note: The approach described here is an abbreviated version of ABC. Whereas conventional ABC methods consider the full range of operating costs, we are only considering direct costs. This eliminates much of the time and complexity associated with the complete approach while retaining our focus on the costs directly associated with process design and performance characteristics.

3.5.1 Establish an Activity Dictionary

The activity dictionary is simply a listing of the activities that comprise your process, where each activity is associated with a value classification code, a driver code, and a cost-of-quality code. The activities and value codes were identified in steps 3.4.1 and 3.4.3. Driver identification simply involves identifying what is causing an activity to be performed. In most cases, the driver will be input volume. Using cost-of-quality coding provides further insight into what is driving process cost. The idea is simply to flag the activities that are performed because there may be an error, there was an error, or we want to prevent errors. The second category may be further refined to identify if an error was externally or internally generated.

3.5.2 Identify Process Resources

Next, we identify the resources that are consumed by the activities. Generally, we limit the resource pool to the human resources performing the process. If time and experience permit, the resource pool can be expanded to include supplies, equipment, and overhead. Since including these categories significantly complicates our work, it is probably best to leave them outside the scope of the initial costing effort.

When the resource pool is determined, we need to identify the cost associated with each resource. For human resources, we generally use the loaded cost (that is, salary plus benefits). We can cost people individually or by position type.

3.5.3 Measure and Allocate Resource Consumption

When we know what the activities and resources are, the next step is to determine the degree of resource consumption associated with each activity. If we are only considering human resources, the task is straightforward since all we have to do is determine where people spend their time. We can accomplish this several ways, including the use of data collection logs, direct observation, or interviews. Although data collection and observation may seem to be the most scientific approaches, interviewing is generally the preferred approach. It is much faster to accomplish and probably no less accurate than the other approaches.

3.5.4 Develop and Evaluate Cost Models

Now that we know the types and amounts of resources that are expended for each activity and the cost of each of the resources, it is a simple matter to estimate the cost associated with each activity. The sum of all of the activity costs describes the total process cost.

By summarizing the costed activities by value classification codes and cost of quality codes, we can gain additional insight into the structure of our process costs. Sometimes, we might be very surprised by how little of the total cost is for value-adding work or by how much of our effort is devoted to preventing, catching, or correcting poor quality.

3.6 SET IMPROVEMENT PRIORITIES

As mentioned previously, phase 4 will focus on implementing the process improvements required to establish a stabilized process. To set the stage for phase 4 work, we need to have a clear understanding of current performance levels and a shared vision of the desired future state of the process. By now we should have a clear understanding of performance from various perspectives.

3.6.1 Identify Improvement Opportunities

Now, we're ready to identify the near-term improvement opportunities that will be tackled in the improve process phase (phase 4) and the standardize process phase (phase 5). The baseline performance data and process goals provide the foundation for conducting this work. When seeking to identify improvement opportunities be sure to:

- Identify and size gaps between performance outcomes and stated process goals.

- Identify and size gaps between performance capabilities and stated process goals.

- Identify and evaluate any current initiatives operating in the same space or on the same issues.

3.6.2 Prioritize Improvement Opportunities

The improvement opportunities identified in the previous step should be evaluated to determine which, if any, should be addressed in the near term and which should be delayed until we resolve basic process infrastructure issues. The primary objective at this point is to determine which road map stage will be used to address each opportunity. If, for example, an issue relates to an acute performance shortfall or defect, we may target resolution for the improve process phase. If it deals with matters of procedure, skills, or compliance, we may chose to incorporate it as part of the standardize process phase. Or, if it deals with manageability of the process, we may slate it for the manage process phase.

3.6.3 Conclude Phase

Before continuing, it's a good idea to formally check in with your sponsors and key stakeholders to validate progress and to ensure you're ready to move to the improve phase. Keeping sponsors and stakeholders informed is essential to maintaining alignment regarding expectations, progress, and future plans.

10

Phase 4, Improve Processes

The primary objectives of the improve process phase are to resolve the key performance gaps that were identified in the baseline phase and to create the stable process environment required to conduct phase 5 work. In this phase we utilize team-based process improvement projects to resolve the priority improvement needs. These initial projects are designed to provide immediate relief from the priority problems while providing the initial training ground for developing organizational competency in process improvement work. Success along both fronts is essential to demonstrating the value of process improvement work.

As shown in Figure 10.1, the improve phase advances maturity level one processes (understood) to level two maturity (stabilized) on the Process Improvement Road Map.

In this chapter we will introduce a foundation methodology to guide our improvement efforts. The methodology, which is a derivative of Six Sigma's DMAIC (define, measure, analyze, improve, and control) approach, can be adapted to handle various types of presenting problems. It begins with an operational problem that requires resolution and guides solution development by uncovering the root causes of the problem and developing solutions that resolve these causes. It asks us to confirm root causes before seeking solutions and to confirm solutions before deploying them. These steps are designed to ensure that our solutions work correctly the first time.

It is important to point out that the methodology is a problem-solving tool. It works within the existing process architecture to address operational problems or needs. It does not question overall process architectures or seek quantum improvements in process capabilities. This type of work falls into

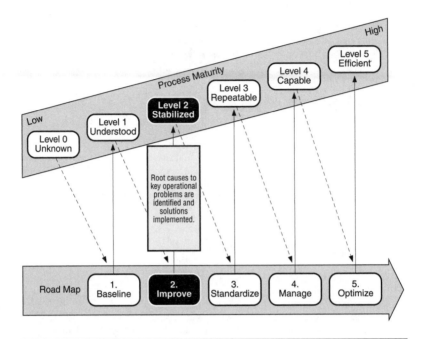

Figure 10.1   The Process Improvement Road Map for systematically advancing process maturity.

the redesign and reengineering categories and is outside the scope of the improve phase.

The outcomes of phase 4 work should be assessed relative to the performance requirements and results that were identified in the baseline phase. Ideally, all of the improvement opportunities identified as near-term improvements in the baseline phase should be completed before leaving phase 4.

4.1 PLANNING AND MANAGING IMPROVEMENT WORK

Process improvement work is generally conducted as team-based project work. Using teams to engage employees who have firsthand knowledge of process operations has the potential to produce higher-quality solutions and more effective solution deployments. To translate this potential into reality, however, teams must be sufficiently skilled and well managed.

Process improvement team members should have a good understanding of improvement methods and tools before they become engaged in process work. Without reasonable skill levels, work quality will suffer and valuable time will be consumed coaching individuals and performing rework. Therefore, it is a good idea to incorporate the process improvement training identified in section 1.5.3 as part of the project launch process.

Good project management practices are also integral to successful process improvement projects. If projects are poorly planned, managed, or concluded, it is unlikely that they will produce the solutions we desire in a timely manner. Figure 10.2 shows how project management practices can be combined with training and methodology to enable effective management of the end-to-end projects. This project management process utilizes three stages to initiate, manage, and conclude projects.

Stage 1, Initiate Project. The initiate project stage begins with a presenting problem or opportunity and concludes with a trained and chartered project team. This is where we evaluate the issue, determine the impacted stakeholders, identify and/or tailor the improvement methodology to meet project needs, set the project team and conduct required training, and prepare the initial project charter. These steps are essential to getting a good start and maintaining clear focus throughout the project. A sample project charter template is included in appendix A.

Stage 2, Manage Project. The manage project stage begins with the charter and methodology from the define project phase and concludes with a validated and deployed solution. Progress relative to the plan should be monitored and reported to sponsoring management on a regular basis. Sponsoring managers are encouraged to actively monitor progress and to occasionally attend project activities to provide support as required.

Stage 3, Conclude Project. This is where we perform the activities required to successfully conclude projects and to ensure that the appropriate

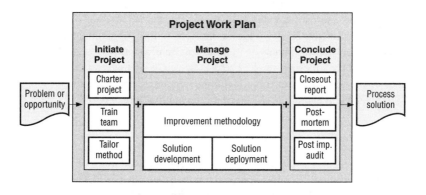

Figure 10.2 The process improvement project management process.

organizational learning occurs. This stage should also include a postimplementation audit to ensure that the improvements were effectively assimilated by the organization and they are delivering expected results. These audits are generally conducted 90 and/or 180 days after deployment. Appendix B includes a simple template to guide postimplementation audits.

4.2 FOUNDATION IMPROVEMENT METHODOLOGY

Figure 10.3 describes the foundation improvement methodology in flowchart form. A quick glance at the flowchart reveals two features of the methodology. First, several of the steps are preceded with decision steps. These decision points allow us to skip steps if the required information has already been developed, thereby shortening solution times. Second, several of the steps conclude with a review to validate that all substeps have been properly completed before moving on to the next step.

The foundation methodology outlines the basic plan of attack for addressing three types of process problems:

1. *Defect elimination.* Something isn't working as it should, the process produces defective outcomes.

2. *Productivity improvement.* The process takes too many resources to produce outcomes.

3. *Lead time reduction.* The process takes too long to execute.

In its standard form, the foundation methodology focuses on the first class of problems. With minor adjustments, however, it can effectively address productivity improvement and lead time reduction work. We will review these adjustments later.

The following briefly reviews the steps in the improvement methodology. The purpose of including this information is simply to provide a high-level sketch of the approach. There is a wealth of material available that describes how to perform the techniques included in the methodology, so there is little reason to replicate that information here.

Step 1, Define Problem

The define step ensures that we have a clear understanding of the presenting problem and the improvements required, and that we have committed to sound action plans for attaining resolution.

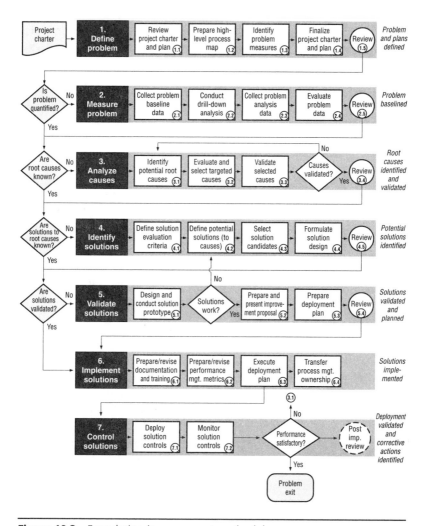

Figure 10.3 Foundation improvement methodology.

1.1 Review Project Charter and Plan. The first step for the project team is to review the draft charter and project plan to understand their contents and to evaluate their completeness, accuracy, and reasonableness.

1.2 Scope Problem Process. It is important to develop a clear understanding of the problem process boundaries and composition very early in the improvement cycle. The first step to developing this information is preparing a high-level process map to scope the solution space and to identify the key subprocesses that operate in the space. The SIPOC tool (a Six Sigma tool) fulfills this purpose nicely.

1.3 Identify Problem Measures. Measurements are essential to helping us detect the presence and/or magnitude of the presenting problem and for establishing performance baselines. It's very important to develop solid consensus regarding the measures that will be used to describe the problem before beginning the data collection work in step 2, Measure Problem.

1.4 Finalize Project Charter and Plan. Now is the time to identify any adjustments to the charter or work plan that may be necessary to ensure project success and to attain mutual commitment. Typical adjustments include project scope, project duration, and participation levels. The adjustments will be reviewed in the next step.

1.5 Conduct Review. Before moving on, the team should meet with the project sponsor to conduct a step review and to confirm any adjustments to the charter or work plan. When this step is exited, the team has contracted with the sponsor to meet the requirements of the charter and plan.

Step 2, Measure Problem

The measure step guides us through our initial measurement work. This work focuses on two types of measurements: (1) problem baseline measurements to quantify the presenting problem and (2) problem analysis measurements to help surface potential root causes to the presenting problem. If the problem is already quantified and there is no need to collect other data, this step may be skipped.

2.1 Collect Problem Baseline Data. It's now time to develop our baselines for the problem measures identified in step 1.3. To prepare for data collection work, it's a good idea to go through the process of developing data collection plans. Data collection planning helps define and design measurements, and develop the procedures to ensure effective collection work.

2.2 Conduct Drill-Down Analysis. Drill-down mapping is a useful tool for narrowing the scope of our analysis and for exposing factors that may help isolate problem sources or causes. In drill-down mapping we practice hierarchical decomposition of process steps to isolate the elements that may be causing the presenting problem.

2.3 Identify and Collect Problem Analysis Measurements. In this step we identify any additional measurements that may help us discover the root causes to the presenting problem. The drill-down mapping work typically points to various possible causes or contributors that warrant early measurement.

2.4 Evaluate Measurement Data. Next, we evaluate the problem baseline and problem analysis data to pinpoint problem locations, sources, frequencies, or patterns. Since it is not uncommon that the answers to our questions prompt more questions, we may find ourselves repeating these measurement steps as we learn more about the process.

2.5 Conduct Review. Before leaving the measure step, a team representative should meet with the project sponsor to review project status and measurement findings. It may be necessary to adjust the team's focus or plans.

Step 3, Analyze Problem Causes

In this step we identify and validate the root causes of the presenting problem. If these causes are known (with a high certainty), the step may be skipped.

3.1 Identify Potential Root Causes. We identify potential root causes of the presenting problem by examining the problem analysis data and detailed maps, and by using the cause-and-effect tool.

3.2 Select Targeted Root Causes. We want to narrow our list of potential causes to the few that are the most likely causes of the presenting problem. Commonly used techniques for narrowing focus include correlation analysis and criteria-based rankings.

3.3 Confirm Root Causes. In this step we determine which of the targeted root causes are the real causes of our problem. The objective is to prove causation empirically. The preferred methods for proving causation are experimentation or observation, although deduction may sometimes be used. If we don't identify the correct causes now, the remaining steps will most likely fail to produce an effective solution to the process problem.

3.4 Conduct Review. Before leaving this step, a team representative should meet with the project sponsor to review project status and findings.

Step 4, Identify Solutions

In this step we identify and select candidate solutions that address confirmed root causes of the presenting problem.

4.1 Define Solution Evaluation Criteria. The first step in solutions work is to define the criteria that will be used to evaluate the suitability of alternative solutions. Commonly considered criteria include: ability to eliminate problem causes (prevention), acceptance, implementation costs, time frames, and risks.

4.2 Identify Potential Solutions. Brainstorming or other creative techniques are generally used to identify potential solutions. This is the time to be creative.

4.3 Select Candidate Solution. Here, we apply the evaluation criteria identified in step 4.1 to score the potential solutions identified in step 4.2 to select the candidate that offers the greatest potential for success.

4.4 Formulate Solution Design. Now that we've identified our candidate solution, we need to draft a solution design that includes sufficient detail to enable validation work. We are not concerned with building or documenting solutions at this time. We are simply concerned with determining how we can validate our solution with the least amount of effort and cost.

4.5 Conduct Review. Before leaving this step, a team representative should meet with the project sponsor to review project status and findings.

Step 5, Validate Solutions

We're now ready to validate the candidate solution to ensure that it resolves the presenting problem (via its root causes). If validation indicates the solution does not work, then another solution should be formulated and tested.

This step is important for two reasons: (1) it ensures that our solution works before we implement it, and (2) it provides us with an estimate of the improvement impact. This improvement impact estimate will help in preparing our business case when we're proposing the solution to stakeholders.

Although this step is sometimes skipped because of time constraints or low-risk assessments, it is advisable to validate our solutions before deploying them.

5.1 Design and Conduct Prototype. The prototype is a trial run or experiment that is designed to confirm our candidate solution. Although prototyping can be somewhat time-consuming and frequently requires large doses of creativity, it is very important work.

5.2 Prepare and Present Improvement Proposal. When we have a confirmed solution, the next step is to sell it to key stakeholders. This is especially important when our solution involves the expenditure of capital or is potentially disruptive to the organization. Even if our solution does not involve these factors, this is the time to update management and to promote our results and efforts.

This is also the time to consider if someone else should be tasked with implementing the solution. Solution development is sometimes separated from deployment for a variety of reasons. Examples might include times when the solution team wants or needs to disband, deployment requires different skills or roles (for example, technology or field), or deployment will take a long time to complete.

5.3 Prepare Deployment Plan. When the solution is approved for deployment, we prepare the solution deployment plan. Generally, this begins with a project work breakdown structure and schedule to organize the steps required to implement our solution.

5.4 Review Deployment Plan. Since the deployment plan will determine the success of our deployment efforts, it's a good idea to conduct a thorough review of the plan with all relevant stakeholders before leaving step 5. One approach to enabling good reviews with minimal disruption involves developing a checklist that describes the characteristics of a good plan. Reviewers are then asked to validate that the plan completely and accurately reflects these characteristics. This approach promotes consistency and thoroughness in the review process while allowing reviewers to work at a time and place that is convenient to them.

Step 6, Implement Solutions

It's now time to implement our solution. If the previous steps were executed appropriately, deployment should be relatively straightforward and your result assured.

6.1 Revise/Prepare Documentation. The impacted process documentation (process description, operating procedures, and training documents) may need to be revised. All proposed changes to process documentation should be approved by the process owner and/or appropriate stakeholders before continuing.

6.2 Revise/Prepare Performance Management Metrics. Existing performance metrics may require revision or new metrics may require development to support the process changes. It is important that we have the required metrics in place to enable effective management of the process as well as to control our solution.

6.3 Execute Deployment Plan. When the documentation and measurements are developed, it's time to execute the rollout portion of our deployment plan. This may involve training and coaching to ensure that performers understand your changes.

6.4 Transfer Ownership. When solution deployment has been completed, it's time to transfer ownership of the process changes to the appropriate oversight personnel (process owner and process management team).

Step 7, Control Solutions

The purpose of this step is to ensure that our solution is sustained and that it continues to mitigate the presenting problem.

7.1 Deploy Controls. Now that our solution is deployed, the question is, how can we know that it continues to perform favorably? To be able to answer this question with confidence, we may need to implement performance metrics that signal the continued deployment and capability of our solution.

7.2 Monitor Controls. Controls are only useful if they are monitored and used. Therefore, it is a good idea to assign someone the responsibility for monitoring the solution controls for a designated period of time. When this period has ended, the process owner should determine if monitoring may be discontinued.

Conclude Project

Although we've completed the improvement methodology, we still need to perform the conclude project stage of the project management process. The key steps in this stage include the closeout report, project postmortem and postimplementation audit. Part III of the sample project charter includes closeout and postimplementation audit sections to guide and record conclusion activities.

4.3 TAILORING THE FOUNDATION METHODOLOGY

As mentioned previously, the foundation methodology can be tailored to handle productivity and time-based problems. The following summarizes these adjustments in narrative form.

Productivity Improvement Adjustments

Step 2, Measure Problem

The measurement strategy for productivity improvement work focuses on determining the amount and value contribution of all resources consumed in process execution. This is accomplished in three steps: (1) mapping the end-to-end process at the activity level, (2) determining the value contribution of each activity, and (3) measuring or estimating the resources consumed by each activity. An activity is defined as a process step that consumes a specific set of resources and is different from its predecessor and successor steps in terms of value contribution (that is, VA, VE, or WW). In other words, when the resources or value contribution change, a new activity is defined.

Step 3, Analyze Causes

The analysis strategy for productivity improvement work involves identifying the drivers of non-value-adding work (VE and WW). Frequent drivers include policies related to reviews and approvals, structures that cause handoffs and transport of work, quality issues that drive inspection, and correction work. The goal is to identify and invalidate the drivers.

Step 4, Identify Solutions

The improvement strategy for productivity involves the following steps: (1) eliminate WW, (2) reduce VE, (3) improve the efficiency of remaining VE, and (4) improve the efficiency of VA.

Lead-Time Reduction Adjustments

Step 2, Measure Problem

The measurement strategy for lead-time reduction focuses on the identification of idle time. This is accomplished in two steps: mapping the end-to-end process to identify all idle and non-idle intervals, and measuring or estimating the duration of each idle time interval. If this strategy doesn't yield a significant component of the total lead time, we may need to measure the activities as well.

Step 3, Analyze Causes

The analysis strategy for lead-time reduction involves identifying the factors that cause work objects to sit around idle. The goal is to identify and eliminate these factors.

Step 4, Identify Solutions

The primary improvement strategy for lead-time reduction is to eliminate idle time. When this is done, the secondary strategy is to follow the steps outlined for productivity improvements.

11

Phase 5, Standardize Processes

In the previous phase we focused on resolving the obvious and urgent improvement needs for our processes. When this work is completed, and our processes are stabilized, we're ready to move on to the standardization phase. The objectives of standardization work are to create processes that are repeatable and reproducible. In this context, repeatable means that our processes are able to produce consistent results, while reproducible means they can be successful duplicated in other locations. Both characteristics are very important in the world of business processes. As shown in Figure 11.1, process standardization advances the maturity of our processes from level 2, Stabilized, to level 3, Repeatable (on the Process Improvement Road Map).

The first step in standardization work is to create a documented process. Documentation is where our process design is translated into actionable and repeatable procedures. Next, we build on the documentation by establishing training and verification programs to ensure the procedures are understood and followed. As we'll soon see, these three elements (documentation, training, and auditing) form a system that enables and sustains desired process behaviors.

Figure 11.2 outlines the steps required to perform the standardization phase.

Since standardization work consumes considerable time and resources, it makes sense to leverage our efforts by incorporating improvements into the standardized process design. The rule of thumb is to incorporate low-risk improvements that can be deployed without requiring significant change to the process architecture or technology platform. If the process warrants

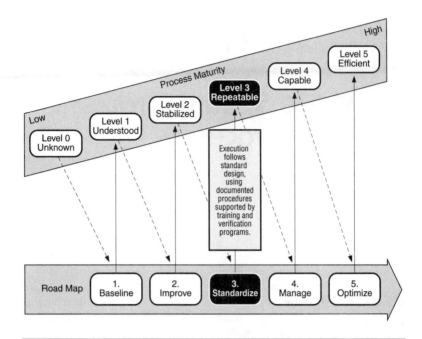

Figure 11.1 The Process Improvement Road Map for systematically advancing process maturity.

major redesign, then we should consider revisiting the improve process phase while using a reengineering methodology. Otherwise, our approach is to seek improvements that are realistic within the existing architecture.

When a process exits the standardize phase, execution is based on a standard design using documented procedures. These procedures are supported by training and verification programs to enable and sustain the design.

INTRODUCING AN INTEGRATED PROCESS AND QUALITY MANAGEMENT SYSTEM

Although process improvement gets the lion's share of attention, process and quality management are equally important disciplines. These disciplines deal with how we ensure the continued capability and efficiency of processes. Traditional approaches to process and quality treat them as separate issues, sometimes involving totally separate management systems. However, the highly interdependent nature of process and quality management warrants a

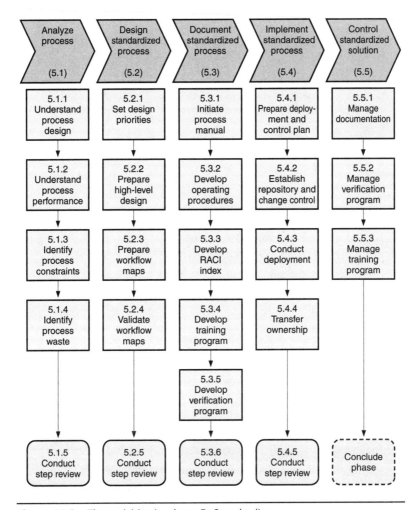

Figure 11.2   The activities in phase 5, Standardize.

single integrated system. When developing a process and quality management system, our approach should be:

- *Complete.* It incorporates good quality and process management practices and it assigns clear roles, responsibilities, and practices.

- *Demonstrable.* It provides verifiable proof of operations as well as outcomes in the form of documentation, records, and data.

- *Integrated.* It is integrated with customer and supplier quality systems, and with our own system of continuous improvement.

- *Sustaining.* It is self policing and self correcting.

- *Managed.* It has clear and viable linkages to operational management.

- *Effective.* It detects and resolves substandard outcomes as well as prevents substandard outcomes.

In this section we will introduce an integrated model for managing process and quality performance. The model is based on a five-level architecture as illustrated in Figure 11.3. The five levels are:

1. *Process management.* Operating at the foundation level, process management forms the operational standards required to manage the key components of processes (inputs, methods, equipment, data, facilities, and people). By establishing clear standards and accountabilities, process management promotes accurate and repeatable execution of the process components.

2. *Process control.* Whereas process management establishes standards for process component execution, process control monitors the performance characteristics of the process component to ensure they are performing appropriately. Process control seeks to determine process outcomes by proactively managing the internal determinants of outcomes using quantitative methods.

3. *Quality control.* Quality control ensures that only quality products are released to customers by using sampling and inspection to assess quality levels of products and services. Samples failing to meet acceptable quality levels are corrected and reevaluated before release to the customer.

4. *Customer acceptance.* This element includes customer practices for determining the acceptability of products and services and for communicating performance feedback to us. Customer acceptance and product quality control practices must be effectively aligned and linked with one another to sustain an effective relationship.

5. *System quality assurance.* Operating at the top level of the model, this element includes the mechanisms required to ensure the continued capability of the overall process and quality management system (levels 1 through 4). Examples of these mechanisms might include process reviews, customer feedback assessment, metrics analysis, and management reviews.

As shown in the model, all five levels are connected to a system of continuous process improvement to ensure that we identify and resolve root causes of operational deficiencies and continuously improve process capability.

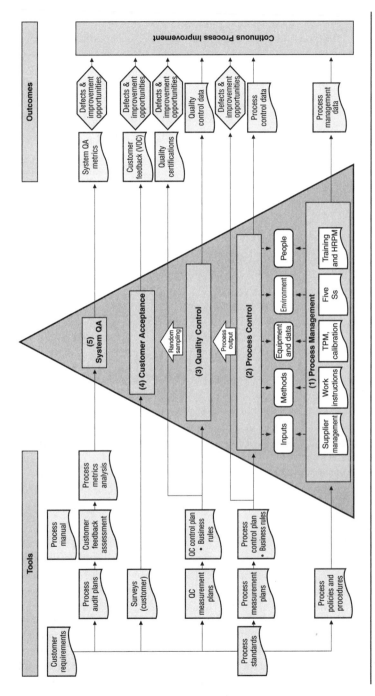

Figure 11.3 The process and quality management system.

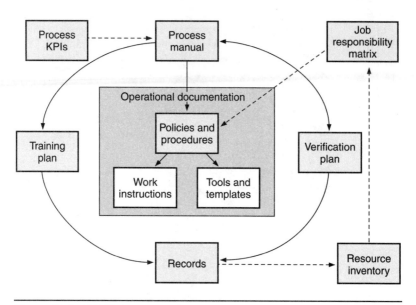

Figure 11.4   PQMS documentation system.

INTRODUCING A PROCESS DOCUMENTATION SYSTEM

Although the process and quality management system model guides us in terms of what to document, it does not guide us in terms of how to document our process. Figure 11.4 provides this guidance by suggesting a documentation architecture. This architecture describes the elements and linkages required to establish a viable and living documentation system for our processes. Later, in phase 6, we will add performance metrics to the documentation component to complete our process and quality management system.

The following describes the components of the process documentation system in greater detail.

Process Manual

The process manual provides a high-level description of the process and the key standards and management practices associated with it. The manual content, size, and level of detail are designed to position it as a customer deliverable. The sections in the process manual are briefly described as follows. A more detailed template is included in appendix C.

• *Process overview.* The overview introduces the process by describing its purpose and relationship to the customers it supports. Here, we describe the key outcomes of the process and how those outcomes contribute to customer value and/or enterprise performance. We also position the process relative to organizational structures (that is, what organizational components participate in the process) and the other processes operating within the enterprise (that is, what are the key process interdependencies). This information is generally communicated via high-level system diagrams. Process ownership and change management practices should also be described in the overview.

• *Process management.* Process management establishes the operational standards required to manage the five process components (that is, inputs, methods, equipment, data, environment, and people). In order to maintain clear linkages to the process and quality management system model, we discuss process management in terms of the individual process components.

– *Inputs.* When process performance is dependent on the quality of its inputs, it is appropriate to establish standard practices for proactively managing inputs. In this section we identify our approaches to managing process inputs. Incoming inspection and supplier management programs are the primary tool sets used in this area.

– *Methods.* Process designs are translated into work methods to enable repeatable execution of designs. The most common approach to managing work methods involves the use of policies and procedures, work instructions, templates, and checklists. In this section we identify our approaches to describing, enabling, and monitoring work methods to ensure they are performed in accordance with process designs.

– *Equipment and data.* Processes generally utilize various types of equipment (ranging from simple hand tools to sophisticated technology) and data. In this section we identify the equipment and data that are used, and the programs that are used to ensure their continued reliability and availability. Commonly used approaches include calibration, preventive maintenance, backups, and disaster recovery programs.

– *Environment.* Processes operate in environments. Relevant environmental factors may include location, work layouts, work arrangements, and ambient conditions. In this section, we identify the programs that are used to ensure that facilities effectively support process work. The *five S* tool set falls into this category.

– *People.* People operate processes using work methods and tools. Therefore, it is appropriate to define how skills are going to be developed and sustained as required to assure effective execution of methods. Commonly used approaches include new employee training, performance assessment, incentive, and certification programs.

• *Process control.* Whereas process management establishes standards for process execution, process control monitors the performance characteristics of the process component to ensure they are performing appropriately. The elements of process control systems are: standards, measurements, and control plans. We will consider process control in much greater detail in phase 6, Institute Process Management.

• *Quality control.* Quality control ensures that only quality products are released to customers by utilizing postprocess sampling and inspection to assess quality levels of products and services. Product populations failing to meet acceptable quality levels are segregated, corrected, and reevaluated before release to the customer. Nonconformances are forwarded to the corrective action system to identify and resolve root causes.

• *Customer quality acceptance.* In this section we describe how process customers determine the acceptability of delivered products and services. It is important to understand how acceptance is determined so that we can design our quality controls systems appropriately. For example, if a customer relies on product certification, it is essential that our product quality control system samples and accepts at the levels required to support certification requirements.

• *System quality assurance.* In this section we describe how we assure the effectiveness of the overall process and quality management system. Commonly used approaches to system quality assurance include metrics and feedback analysis, process reviews, and management reviews.

• *Continuous process improvement.* In this section we describe how each of the five levels of the process and quality management system are connected to continuous process improvement. Without visible and active connections between these systems, it is unlikely that process improvement will ever become integrated into the fabric of normal business operations.

Job Responsibility Matrix

The job responsibility matrix identifies operational procedure responsibilities by job (see Figure 11.5). A job is a role that may be occupied by one or more people and will generally be associated with multiple operating procedures. Each procedure that is associated with a job is assigned one of the following codes to indicate the nature of the responsibility:

Procedures	Jobs												
	Job A	Job B	Job C	Job D	Job E	Job F	Job G	Job H	Job I	Job J	Job K	Job L	Job M
Procedure 1		R		A			I				I	I	
Procedure 2			R	A			I						
Procedure 3	I			A		R					I		
Procedure 4	I							A	R			I	
Procedure 5	R					I		A					
Procedure 6			R			I		A					
Procedure 7							I	A			R	I	
Procedure 8		R		A			I				I		
Procedure 9				A	R							I	
Procedure 10	I			A	I							R	
Procedure 11	I		R	A	I								
Procedure 12				A	I		R						

R = Responsible for performing procedure
A = Accountable for ensuring procedure is executed appropriately
I = Responsible for remaining informed regarding procedure execution

Figure 11.5   The job responsibility matrix.

R = Responsible, to indicate the job is responsible for performing the procedure

A = Accountable, to indicate the job is responsible for ensuring the procedure is performed properly

I = Informed, to indicate the job is responsible for staying informed regarding performance of the procedure

The responsibility for the content of operating procedures is defined in the procedures themselves.

Operational Documentation

The operational documentation component of our process documentation contains the information required to execute the process. Three types of operational document are generally used:

• *Policies and procedures.* Policies and procedures describe set operating accountabilities by describing who does what.

- *Work instructions.* Work instructions are used to supplement policies and procedures when it is necessary to describe specifically how work steps are to be performed. Work instructions are generally reserved for more complicated work steps.

- *Tools and templates.* Tools and templates include the various tools (for example, checklists) and templates (for example, blank forms) that are used when performing procedures and instructions.

Training Plan

The training plan describes how and how often skills will be assessed and how skills are developed. The process owner is responsible for establishing a systematic approach to process-related training. This includes the development, deployment, and management of training materials and records. Operating managers may be responsible for conducting performance reviews and training interventions.

Verification Plan

The verification plan is used to describe how and how often compliance to procedures and instructions is verified, and how verification results are used to drive corrective action.

Records

Records are maintained to document training interventions and results and verification reviews and results. Records are integral to maintaining accountability required to sustain long-term viability of the system.

INTRODUCING A DOCUMENTATION MANAGEMENT SYSTEM

Process documentation must be managed to ensure that process participants are aware of and have access to current information. Figure 11.6 illustrates a simple process documentation management system. In this system, users are provided full inquiry access to the documentation repository. Changes are coordinated by the repository librarian, who is the only person with update authority. Changes are handled as follows. Anyone can initiate a change request by forwarding their request to the librarian. The librarian forwards the request to the content owner for evaluation and possible implementation. Content ownership is established for each artifact maintained in

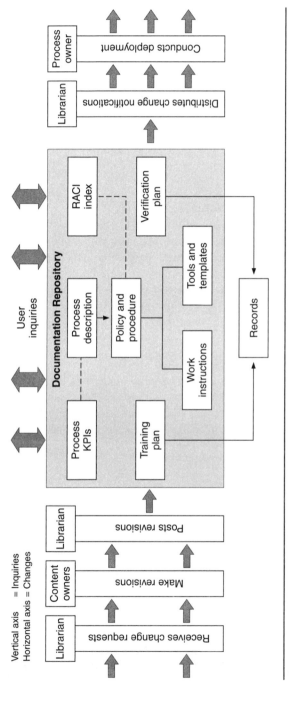

Figure 11.6 Documentation management system.

the repository by the process owner. Content owners communicate with requestors to obtain relevant information and to communicate the disposition of requests. Content revisions are prepared by the content owner and forwarded to the process owner for review and approval. The process owner forwards approved revisions to the librarian for posting to the repository. The librarian distributes change notices to all positions identified in the job responsibility matrix to positively inform process participants of the change.

The following describes the steps for conducting process standardization work.

5.1 ANALYZE PROCESS

Before beginning standardization work, it is important to have a clear understanding of the process design, operations, and performance. The baseline phase included the analysis work required to generate this information. If baselining was not performed, however, or if the information generated is no longer current, it may be prudent to revisit the first three steps of the baseline phase before entering this step.

5.1.1 Understand Process Design

The first step is to develop an adequate understanding of the existing process design and operations. The process workflow maps generated during the baseline phase provide the foundation for developing this understanding. It is a good idea to validate the maps if significant time has passed since they were created or if many process changes were deployed during the improve phase.

5.1.2 Understand Process Performance

Next, we review the performance data generated during the baseline phase to understand the relative importance of the performance dimensions, as well as the dimensions that are underperforming. Be sure to adjust the baseline data to reflect any changes that were produced during the improve phase.

5.1.3 Identify Process Constraints

Review the process to identify the primary constraints to flow. This can be accomplished by observing the process to identify buildups of work in process or the steps or handoffs involving long delays. These constraints to flow offer potential opportunities to improve the velocity of the process.

5.1.4 Identify Process Waste

Review the process to identify opportunities for waste reduction. Work steps that were classified as waste work during the baseline phase are the obvious candidates for elimination in the standardized process. Also consider the steps that include rework, error detection, or correction processing, or that involve handoffs or delays. By identifying and eliminate the drivers of this work we can improve the efficiency of the standardized process.

5.2 DESIGN STANDARD PROCESS

Now that we've developed an understanding of current process operations and capabilities, we're ready to begin designing the standardized process. Our objective is to develop a process solution that seeks to address known process limitations without radically reengineering the process architecture or technology platform.

5.2.1 Set Design Priorities

Setting design priorities helps the design team resolve focus around mutually agreed objectives. For example, if the team is seeking to improve process quality, the design effort will incorporate techniques designed to prevent and detect defective outcomes. If the team is seeking to reduce cycle time, however, the design effort will focus on identifying and eliminating constraints and idle time throughout the process.

5.2.2 Prepare High-Level Design

Draft a high-level view of the new process architecture. This high-level view should describe the key subprocesses that will comprise the process and the work products they produce. Subprocesses should have clearly delineated boundaries and outcomes, and should not be reiterated once they are exited. Also identify the key process and system interfaces and the organizational units that will participate in the process.

5.2.3 Prepare Workflow Maps

When the high-level design work is completed, the next step is to define the workflow maps for the subprocesses that comprise the business process. These maps should be prepared at the level of detail required to support the development of operating procedures. Generally, mapping at the who-does-what level is sufficient to drive procedure preparation.

A few tips to consider when preparing the workflow maps include:

- Strive for a clean design that has clear boundaries and flow. Avoid circuitous flows and backtracking.

- Sequence work steps in their logical order. Sometimes process steps are worked out of order in an effort to gain speed, which produces complex or unmanageable processes.

- Identify the points within the process where quality, efficiency, or flow need to be safeguarded. Incorporate controls at these points to mange these risks.

- When seeking to reduce cycle time, focus on improving the throughput of constraints and eliminating idle time.

- When seeking to improve productivity, focus on eliminating or reducing non-value-adding work steps. Identify and minimize rework and handoffs and consider combining work steps. Apply technology only after the process has been streamlined.

- When seeking to improve quality, focus on defect prevention and upstream defect detection as the preferred strategies. Use postprocess inspection when quality cannot be ensured upstream.

5.2.4 Validate Workflow Maps

Validate the new workflow maps with the people who perform the work to ensure that the design is viable from their perspective. This review should be conducted at a low level of detail to flush out any operational issues that may be present. Expect to make changes as a result of these reviews.

Next, review the design with operational managers to validate the integrity and sufficiency of the design. Be sure to consider the manageability of the process and its relationship with other processes when conducting the management review sessions. Manageability includes the ability to know and control quality and performance at key points along the process lifecycle as well as at the end of the process.

5.3 DOCUMENT STANDARDIZED PROCESS

When we have a validated design for the standardized process, we're ready to begin documenting the design. This includes development of all of the components shown in Figure 11.4. When we're done, we will have all of the tools needed to effectively enable and sustain execution to the standardized design.

5.3.1 Initiate Process Manual

The process manual is the primary policy document for the process. Key elements of the manual include high-level summary information, performance standards and metrics, quality and performance management practices, and operational practices. Although we cannot complete the manual at this time, this is the time to initiate development. A manual template is included in appendix C.

5.3.2 Develop Operational Documentation

Operational documentation includes the policies and procedures, work instructions, and tools and templates required to enable consistent execution of the standardized process.

1. *Policies and procedures.* Develop operational polices and procedures that reflect the workflow defined in the workflow diagrams. Writing procedures at the who-does-what level provides the level of detail required to provide effective guidance and to establish task-level accountabilities. When writing procedures for large cross-functional processes, it may be helpful to separate procedures by functional units.

2. *Work instructions.* In situations where who does what does not provide sufficient guidance, work instructions may be established to define specifically how tasks are to be performed. Each work instruction must be linked to a specific step in a parent policy and procedure.

3. *Tools and templates.* Tools and templates are developed to guide and enable process execution. The most common items in this category include checklists, flowcharts, and blank forms. Each tool and template must be linked to a specific policy and procedure.

5.3.3 Develop Job Responsibility Matrix

The job responsibility matrix is used to identify the various levels of accountability associated with the operational policies and procedures. Later, this information will be used as the basis for verifying compliance and understanding of policies and procedures, targeting training and communicating changes.

5.3.4 Develop Training Program

One of the keys to deploying and sustaining the standardized process is an effective training program. The program should communicate process-level information (such as scope, goals and measurements, architecture, interfaces and interdependencies, and supporting systems) to all process performers and stakeholders, while also communicating the operational details (such as operating policies and procedures, work instructions, and tools and templates) to the performers.

Initially, the program is used as the means to communicate the details of the standardized process to process performers. Subsequently, the program is used on an ongoing basis to orient new employees and for refresher training for existing employees as needed.

5.3.5 Develop Verification Program

We've all seen situations where new procedures were developed and communicated, only to find out later that the changes didn't seem to take hold. We may find that process performers are continuing old or individual practices, and that the documentation is simply collecting dust. The challenge is to ensure that the standardized process does take hold and that the documentation has meaning to process performers.

The key to ensuring compliance with the standardized process is to conduct ongoing reviews of operating practices to verify that performers understand and follow the process. Conducting these reviews communicates a strong message that compliance is expected. It also generates important feedback regarding the effectiveness of the process design, training materials and methods, and the deployment of process improvements.

5.4 IMPLEMENT STANDARDIZED PROCESS

In this phase we plan and conduct deployment of the standardized process.

5.4.1 Prepare Deployment and Control Plans

A deployment project plan should be developed to coordinate deployment efforts. Deployment planning generally begins by developing a project work breakdown structure (WBS) that identifies and related the tasks required to conduct deployment. Resources and dates are assigned to these tasks as the basis for determining the project schedule. It's essential that the plan includes the appropriate levels of training to ensure that all stakeholders and performers understand the operating policies and procedures.

5.4.2 Establish Documentation Repository and Change Control System

Process documentation must be controlled to safeguard its integrity while it must also be readily available to all performers. Earlier, we introduced a simple approach to addressing the documentation management and change control needs for our process and quality management system. It's now time to implement this or other appropriate methods for maintaining and changing documentation.

5.4.3 Conduct Deployment

We're now ready to begin deploying the standardized process. It may be a good idea to conduct a controlled deployment before rolling out the full deployment plan. A controlled deployment is simply a phased approach, where parts of the solution are phased in over time or where we initially deploy solutions in small areas of the organization. Using a controlled deployment approach provides us the opportunity to test the sufficiency of the solution and deployment plan and to make adjustments before embarking on large-scale change.

5.4.4 Transfer Ownership

When the standardized process has been deployed, the standardization team may disengage from the project and ownership is transitioned to the process owner.

5.5 CONTROL STANDARDIZED PROCESS

Now that the standardized process has been fully deployed, we are ready to begin the business of monitoring compliance and training.

5.5.1 Manage Process Documentation

The repository and change control system established in step 5.4.2 provides continued access and integrity for all process documentation. The repository owner has primary responsibility for managing this system.

5.5.2 Manage Training Program

The training program defined in step 5.3.4 must be managed to ensure that training is conducted for new employees and employees identified as requiring refresher training via the verification program. The process owner has primary responsibility for managing this program.

5.5.3 Manage Verification Program

Verification reviews should be scheduled and conducted as appropriate to provide confidence that operating practices are followed and understood by process performers. These reviews may signal the need for refresher training, corrective action, or changes to the process design. It is essential that the review process be institutionalized. This generally involves the establishment of an audit schedule and competent audit team. The process owner should have primary responsibility for managing this program.

Standardization Wrap-Up

When we have completed the steps outlined above, we will have developed and deployed the foundations for operating a standardized process. By developing process standards and the supporting systems that enable and monitor performance to those standards, we have set the conditions for a repeatable process. Now that we have the levers in place that enable us to control process practices, we can begin our pursuit of process capability in phase 6.

12

Phase 6, Institute Process Management

In phase 5 we developed a standardized process model and the management tools (procedures, training, and audits) that enable us to influence process execution on a continuing basis. Establishing these tools makes it possible for us to ensure conformance to standard process designs as well as to adjust the designs when they are not meeting performance requirements. In phase 6 we will add the navigational systems required to tell us when process performance is on course or when adjustments are required. It is by coupling the ability to know current process performance with the ability to control process execution that we establish the means to attain and sustain capable business processes.

In chapter 3 we introduced process capability as a statistical concept that estimates the ability of processes to produce favorable outcomes. In order to develop these estimates, phase 6 focuses on establishing the measurement systems required to support statistical process control techniques.

As shown in Figure 12.1, successful completion of this work advances the process maturity of our processes to level 4 (Capable) on the Process Improvement Road Map.

INTRODUCING A MEASUREMENT MODEL

Measurement is integral to business process management. Without measurement, it is impossible to effectively manage process performance, or worse, it is impossible to even know if performance is satisfactory. The

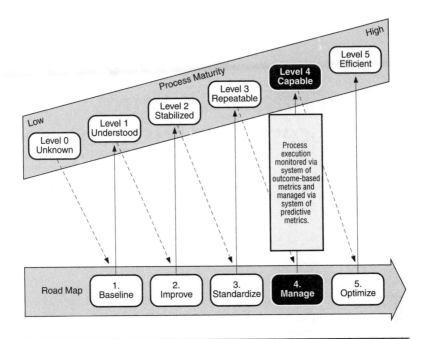

Figure 12.1 The Process Improvement Road Map for systematically advancing process maturity.

fundamental relevance of measurement is expressed via the following adage: "You cannot improve that which you cannot manage, you cannot manage that which you cannot control, and you cannot control that which you don't measure."

Although the importance of measurement is widely acknowledged, it is rare to see effective and complete measurement systems in operation. Contributing factors may range from a hesitancy to engage in activities that do not promise immediate paybacks to a lack of understanding of how measurement systems are developed. In this phase we seek to mitigate the second factor by presenting a simple measurement model that meets the needs of business process management.

The model approaches process measurement in two stages. The first stage establishes a system of measurements that measure process outcomes relative to process goals. The measurements established in this stage are called process outcome measures. The second stage builds on the first by adding a system of measurements that enables proactive management of process outcomes. The measurements established in this stage are called process driver measures.

Measuring Process Outcomes

In stage one, measurements are used to gauge how effectively processes meet process level goals (see Figure 12.2). The class of measurements used in this stage view business processes as *black boxes*. That is to say, they are only concerned with process outcomes, not with how processes perform internally. Since the measurements in this class are only able to describe performance after it occurs, they are also referred to as *trailing indicators*.

Although process outcome measurements may be used in conjunction with feedback systems to guide process adjustments, they are not positioned as proactive process management tools. Instead, they are simply positioned as indicators of the capability of processes to meet process-level goals.

Managing Process Outcomes

Managing process outcomes is about cause and effect. Here, our objective is to identify the internal performance factors that determine process outcomes and to proactively manage those factors. Of course, performance drivers must have solid causal linkages to the process outcomes they are designed to predict.

Figure 12.3 illustrates the second measurement stage. The measurements used in stage two work inside business processes to manage the factors that

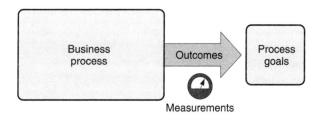

Figure 12.2 Measuring process outcomes.

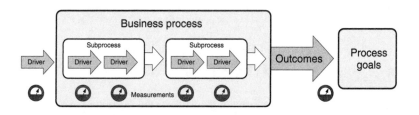

Figure 12.3 Managing process outcomes.

determine process outcomes. Since these measurements precede process outcomes they are also referred to as *leading indicators*.

Managing process drivers is about understanding and managing variation. This means that driver-related measurements should be recorded and analyzed in specific ways. Generally, this means they should be recorded as time-series variable data and with sufficient frequency to be able to identify problems before they translate to inappropriate process outcomes.

A Caution About Measurement

Instituting process measurements will influence people's perceptions and behaviors. These influences are not limited to the people who are directly impacted by the measurements; they may well involve much larger organizational expanses.

How measurements are perceived will have a major impact on how effectively they are used and how long they are sustained. It is important, therefore, that we proactively manage these perceptions by communicating the purpose of measurements, how they will and will not be used, and even the results that are produced. These communications must come from enterprise leadership and must be repeated regularly and consistently.

An Implementation Plan

Figure 12.4 outlines the steps for implementing the measurement model. The first two steps in this plan describe the activities associated with implementing process outcome measurements, while the third and fourth steps describe the activities associated with implementing process performance driver measurements. The final step involves integrating process metrics into the enterprise dashboard.

Since phase 6 is positioned as a start-up phase, we only describe the activities related to implementing process measurements in the following plan. The activities associated with utilizing and maintaining our measurements will be described later in phase 7, which is an ongoing operational phase.

6.1 DESIGN PROCESS OUTCOME METRICS

The following steps (6.1.1 through 6.1.4) describe planning work that was covered in previous phases. If that work was conducted completely and if the outcomes of that work remain current, steps 6.1.1 through 6.1.4 may be

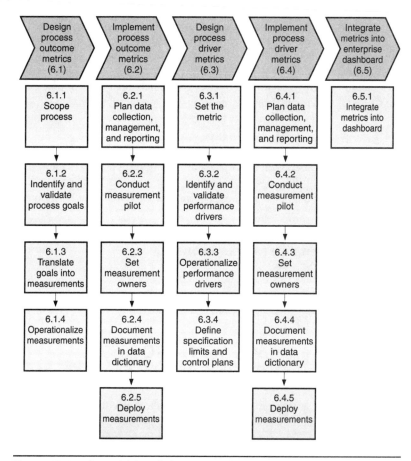

Figure 12.4 The activities of phase 6, Implementing Process Management Metrics.

skipped. Since substantial time and learning may have occurred since phase 2 and 3 work was performed, however, it is a good idea to revisit this important planning work.

6.1.1 Clarify Process Scope and Context

We must begin with clear and mutually accepted process boundaries before venturing into measurement work. In step 3.2.1 we discussed process scoping as the way to set boundaries. If that work was performed completely and its outcomes remain appropriate, this step can be skipped. Otherwise, revisit step 3.2.1.

6.1.2 Validate Process Goals

Since process measurement begins with goals, it's essential to begin with the right goals in mind. In step 2.3 we discussed setting process goals in significant detail. If that work was performed completely and the resulting goals are still appropriate, this step can be skipped. Otherwise, revisit step 2.3.

6.1.3 Translate Goals into Measurements

In step 3.3.2 we discussed how to use the goal–question–metric method to convert our goals into measurements. If that work was performed completely and its outcomes remain appropriate, this step can be skipped. Otherwise, revisit step 3.3.2.

6.1.4 Operationalize Measurements

In step 3.3.3 we discussed the steps for operationalizing measurements. If that work was performed completely and its outcomes remain appropriate, this step can be skipped. Otherwise, revisit step 3.3.3.

6.2 IMPLEMENT PROCESS OUTCOME METRICS

Now that we've identified what we need to measure, the next step is to determine how our measurements will be implemented. The following steps guide us through measurement implementation work.

6.2.1 Plan Data Collection and Management

The first consideration when planning the implementation of process measurements is whether the data will be collected, managed, and reported manually or via automation. Although the approach used will have a significant impact on how things operate, the following planning steps should be thoroughly considered regardless of the approach used.

- *Plan data collection.* Consider the following questions when planning data collection:

  - Where are the data coming from? What systems, locations, people, and so on, may be involved?

  - Is data preparation required? If so, what kinds and who is responsible?

- Are any conversions or translations required? If so, what are they and who owns them?

- Is validation required? If so, what are the validation rules and who owns or performs them?

- Who owns the data collection activity (irrespective of automated or manual methods)?

The answers to these questions should be appropriately documented in written operating procedures.

- *Plan data management.* Questions to consider when planning data management include:

  - Where will the data will be stored (for example, file cabinet, computer, warehouse, and so on)?

  - What security measures, if any, apply to the data?

  - How long will the data be stored?

  - Who owns the stored data?

  - Who owns the supporting documentation and procedures?

The answers to these questions should be appropriately documented in written operating procedures.

- *Plan data analysis and reporting.* Questions to consider when planning data analysis and reporting include:

  - What gets reported to whom and when?

  - What conditions determine what gets reported?

  - How are screens and reports formatted (graphs, narratives, spreadsheets, slides, and so on)?

  - How are data disseminated (online, hard copy, mail, e-mail, and so on)?

The answers to these questions should be appropriately documented in written operating procedures.

6.2.2 Conduct Measurement Pilot

It's important to pilot our measurement procedures and/or systems in real life (including the methods for collecting, recording, and analyzing data). Piloting will test the feasibility of the process and discover problems with the resulting data.

6.2.3 Set Measurement Owners

Every measurement should be assigned to a measurement owner. The owner is responsible for ensuring that measurement data are collected, prepared, managed, analyzed, and reported properly. While these tasks may be delegated to various jobs (via the R designation in the job responsibility matrix), the accountability for these tasks should reside with the measurement owner (via an A designation in the job responsibility matrix).

6.2.4 Document Measurements in a Data Dictionary

All measurement-related definitions should be recorded in a central data dictionary.

6.2.5 Deploy Measurements

When we've conducted a successful measurement pilot, we're ready to prepare and execute a measurement deployment plan. In addition to describing the steps and timing for implementation, the plan should cover any training that is required to ensure effective understanding of the procedures, tools, or statistical techniques required to administer the measurement system. It may also be helpful to establish an ongoing support function to assist with resolving questions or problems as they occur.

6.3 DESIGN PROCESS DRIVER METRICS

The following steps (6.3.1 through 6.3.4) describe the steps for designing process driver metrics. These four steps need to be repeated for each process outcome measurement (POM) we desire to manage via performance driver metrics. Due to the amount of work involved, it's a good idea to limit this population to the vital few POMs that are integral to attaining the key process outcome goals.

6.3.1 Set the Metric

First we select the POMs that we want to proactively manage. For each POM we select, the following steps should be performed.

6.3.2 Identify and Validate Process Drivers

Brainstorm a list of the factors that may determine or influence the results of the selected POM. It is helpful to use the cause-and-effect technique when conducting this brainstorming, since we are seeking to identify causal relationships. The factors identified in this way are potential process driver measurements (PDMs).

Remember that POMs are trailing indicators of process results, while PDMs are internally focused measures of the factors that determine those outcomes. An example may illustrate further: A POM for a customer servicing process may be the percentage of on-time service appointments. The associated PDMs may include appointment lead times, accuracy of addresses, or service representative schedule saturation. By managing these drivers within acceptable levels, the resulting on-time service levels are proactively managed.

When identifying PDMs consider the following criteria:

- Are they sensitive to the POM they are predicting?

- Can they be paired with specific POM results?

- Can they be plotted over time?

- Are they easy to understand?

- Are they easy to obtain?

Figure 12.5 provides an example of how POM and PDM information may be organized.

PDMs should be validated to ensure they have meaningful predictive value. The preferred method of validation is regression analysis to statistically

Business Process	Process Outcome Measurement (POM)	Work Process	Process Driver Measurement (PDM)
Customer service order fulfillment	Schedule attainment rate—the rate of appointments scheduled as requested to total number of appointments booked.	Service order entry	Cycle time from customer order entry to customer representative working order
			Appointment request quality level
			Lead time from request receipt to requested appointment time
	Appointment attainment rate—the ratio of appointments met to number of appointments scheduled.	Service delivery point	Field service representative schedule saturation level
			Planned appointment durations versus actuals
			Planned transit times versus actuals

Figure 12.5 A sample form organizing POM and PDM information.

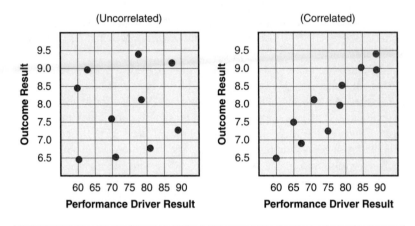

Figure 12.6   Regression analysis of outcome and performance driver results.

evaluate the strength of the relationships operating between potential drivers and process outcomes (see Figure 12.6). This may be accomplished by using historical data or experimentation.

If these choices are not available or practical, or if the relationships are intuitively obvious, it may make sense to implement the performance driver and validate the linkages after data collection has been in operation for a time.

Regardless of the approach used, it is important to monitor the relationships between paired outcome and driver measurements over time.

6.3.3 Operationalize Performance Drivers

Each process performance driver needs to be operationalized to ensure it is properly and consistently understood and used. The following tips supplement the guidance offered in section 3.3.3 for operationalizing measurements.

Recording frequency. When establishing the measurement frequency for performance drivers, it is a good idea to consider: (1) the process turnover rate, (2) the reaction time before consequences are incurred, and (3) the need for statistical significance. Generally, performance drivers should be measured more frequently than performance outcomes.

Recording format. Performance drivers should be recorded using variable (ratio) point data that records individual observations along a time series. Summarized data (MTD or YTD) cannot be used for performance drivers.

6.3.4 Define Specification Limits and Control Plans

Specification limits and control plans make our process driver measurement data actionable. Specification limits describe the acceptable range of behavior. They may be bilateral (using both lower and upper limits) or unilateral (using either upper or lower limits). Later, we will see how specifications are used to determine process capability.

Measurement results that exceed specification limits should trigger the implementation of control plans. Control plans describe the immediate and long-term responses that are invoked when results exceed specification limits or when a process exhibits an out of control condition (discussed later). A sample process management control plan is included in appendix D.

6.4 IMPLEMENT PROCESS DRIVER METRICS

The steps for implementing process driver measurements are the same as those for implementing process outcome measurements (see section 6.2).

6.5 INTEGRATE PROCESS MEASURES INTO ENTERPRISE PERFORMANCE DASHBOARD

The process owner should ensure that key process outcome measurements are incorporated into the enterprise performance dashboard. The dashboard provides an effective vehicle for integrating measurement goals and results using summary or exception techniques. A well-designed and deployed dashboard encourages organizationwide focus on the vital few measurements and promotes accountability for their outcomes. It's a good idea to expose people to statistical process control (SPC) principles to enable proper interpretation of any trend data that might be included in the dashboard.

13

Phase 7, Manage Processes

We're now ready to enter the first ongoing operational phase in the transformation strategy. Whereas the previous phases were presented as projects (with beginnings and endings), the remaining phases describe ongoing functions (that have no endings).

Phase 7 is positioned as the process management phase. The key activities in this phase include: managing process results, managing the supporting process management programs, documentation and training, and ensuring the continued alignment between process and enterprise goals and structures.

Figure 13.1 outlines the high-level activities that comprise the manage process phase. Notice that the steps positioned in the upper region of the diagram relate to managing process performance, the steps positioned in the middle region relate to managing process goals and systems alignment, and the steps positioned in the lower region relate to maintaining the measurements and their supporting documentation and training. All of these steps can initiate process improvement work.

7.1 MONITOR PROCESS OUTCOME RESULTS

Since processes exist to produce outcomes, we should proactively monitor these outcomes to ensure continued compliance with performance standards. The primary ongoing responsibilities associated with monitoring follow.

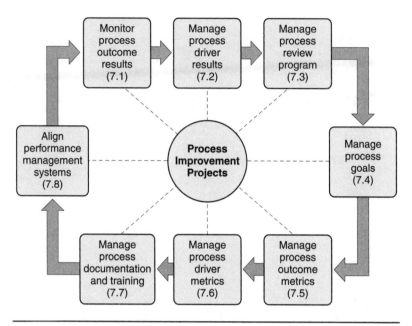

Figure 13.1   The activities in phase 7, Manage Processes.

7.1.1 Monitor Process Performance

In step 6.2 we established measurement owners for our process measurements. The measurement owners should be tasked with the primary responsibility for regularly monitoring measurement results, verifying their continued compliance with performance standards, and detecting unfavorable trends that may be evolving.

7.1.2 Dispatch Process Improvements

The measurement owners should cause investigations to be performed when unfavorable results or trends are observed. It is important that we use fact-based analysis techniques to conduct these investigations. Deficiencies of sufficient magnitude or complexity may warrant the initiation of formal process improvement projects.

• *Check drivers.* Determine if the performance deficiency was signaled by supporting driver measurements. If the existing drivers failed to signal the outcome deficiency, then we should consider adopting a new driver measurement as part of corrective action planning.

• *Avoid misinterpretations.* Misinterpreting measurement results can cause serious problems. Frequently, observers conclude that fluctuations in process outcome measurements are signaling a significant operational change. If the change is perceived as positive, we may conclude that something good has happened and reward ourselves appropriately. Or, if the change is perceived as negative, we may conclude that a process adjustment is warranted. Either of these responses may be totally unwarranted if the fluctuation is simply normal process variation. Unnecessary tampering with processes generally worsens the performance it was intended to improve.

7.2 MANAGE PROCESS DRIVER RESULTS

The following steps offer guidance for using process driver measures to proactively manage process performance.

7.2.1 Monitor Driver Stability

Since process drivers are positioned as predictors of outcomes, our process management strategy is to monitor the stability and capability of the drivers. We accomplish this by applying SPC techniques to the performance driver data. Although some degree of training in SPC is helpful, the techniques are simple to understand and easy to apply.

In simple terms, SPC does two things: (1) it monitors process control and (2) it estimates process capability. A process is said to be in control when it operates in a *statistically* stable manner. Since a stable process operates within a predictable range of behavior, it is frequently called a *repeatable* process. The key to maintaining repeatability is to identify and remove the causes of any nonnormal (or special cause) variation that may appear in a process. The normally expected variation that describes the predictable range of behavior is called *common cause variation.*

The presence of special cause variation indicates that a process is out of statistical control, and that corrective action is needed to identify and eliminate the cause. By catching an out-of-control condition early, it is possible to correct internal process problems before they adversely impact process outcomes.

Process control charts (see Figure 13.2) are used to monitor the variation operating in processes. It is important to note that being in control does not mean a process is capable of producing desired results. As you can see, the process control chart does not consider process specifications.

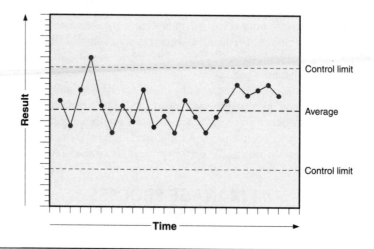

Figure 13.2   A sample process control chart.

7.2.2 Monitor Driver Capability

A process is said to be *capable* when it is stable (in control) and operates within the desired performance range (within specification limits). Capability is determined by the width of the process variation relative to the specification range and the degree of centering present (see Figure 13.3). A capable process will produce desired results 99.7 percent of the time without intervention (based on ±3 standard deviation units).

7.2.3 Dispatch Process Improvements

Process control or capability problems warrant investigation based on structured, fact-based methods that discover and eliminate the root causes of operational problems.

7.3 MANAGE PROCESS REVIEW PROGRAM

Initiation of a compliance and skills review program was described in step 5.5. Once established, the process owner should be responsible for sustaining the program by scheduling, planning, and conducting reviews on a regular basis. The process council should review audit schedules, methods, and results to ensure continued program integrity.

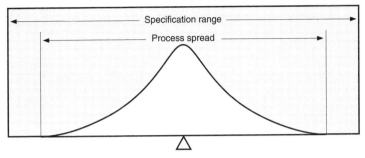

Capable processes:
- Do not produce nonconformances
- Reduce waste and rework
- Increase capacity
- Require less inspection
- Are in control

Figure 13.3 Describing process capability. Variation determines the capability of processes.

7.4 MANAGE PROCESS GOALS

Since process performance is ultimately judged based on process goals, it is important that we systematically maintain our process goals to ensure they continue to reflect the appropriate performance dimensions at the right levels and that they remain aligned with enterprise strategy. The process council should conduct reviews of all business process goals at least quarterly.

7.5 MANAGE PROCESS OUTCOME METRICS

7.5.1 Manage Measurement Documentation

Measurement definitions and documentation should be managed in a central repository under the control of a designated repository owner. Under this approach, all changes to measurement documentation can be funneled to the repository owner for controlled distribution and maintenance. Ownership of the documentation and tools that are maintained in the repository should reside with those owning the measurements, however, not with the repository owner.

7.5.2 Manage Measurement Data

Each measurement item should have an owner who is responsible for ensuring that the data are collected and managed appropriately and securely. The measurement owner should be identified in the data dictionary.

7.6 MANAGE PROCESS DRIVER METRICS

7.6.1 Manage Measurement Documentation

The measurement documentation for process driver measurements should be managed the same as the documentation for process outcome measures.

7.6.2 Manage Measurement Data

The measurement data for process drivers should be managed the same as the data for process outcome measures.

7.6.3 Manage Measurement Relationships

The relations between paired process outcome measures and process driver measures should be regularly monitored to ensure that meaningful correlations continue to operate.

This may be accomplished by conducting regression analysis on measurement pairs to evaluate the sufficiency of these relationships (see Figure 13.4). A more sophisticated statistical technique, called analysis of variance, can also be used to examine the nature and strength of the relationships operating between several variables simultaneously.

Of course, process performance drivers that do not provide sufficient predictive value should be discontinued and new, more effective measures identified.

7.7 MANAGE PROCESS DOCUMENTATION AND TRAINING

Since operational documentation and training are integral components of the organization's performance management systems, it is essential that they are maintained in alignment with process and organizational best practices and

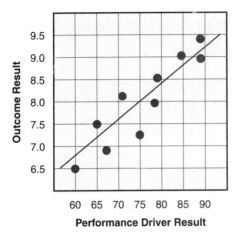

Figure 13.4 Monitoring relationships using regression analysis.

goals. The process owner should be responsible for establishing and maintaining the systems needed to maintain process documentation and training.

7.8 ALIGN AND MANAGE PERFORMANCE MANAGEMENT SYSTEM

Process Performance Management

Historically, process worker performance has been evaluated based on functionally derived performance goals (goals deployed via organizational charts). In the process-focused organization, however, job and individual performance goals and work standards must support end-to-end process needs. Therefore, the process owner must continuously work with the functional managers who support the process to ensure that job and departmental goals are maintained in alignment with the overarching process goals. When misalignments cannot be resolved at this level, the process owner should escalate them to the process council for resolution.

In addition to ensuring continued goal alignment, the process owner must ensure that goal-related measurement data are collected, recorded, and used to track process performance relative to goals.

Enterprise Performance Dashboard

The process owner should ensure that accurate process goals and related performance data are supplied to the enterprise performance dashboard on a regular basis. Without timely and accurate performance data, the dashboard will not be a viable management tool for enterprise managers.

14

Phase 8, Optimize Processes

The objective of the optimization phase is to attain a state of continuous improvement. After all, it is only by continuously improving performance that we can effectively respond to the increasing value expectations of our customers and the competitive challenges of the marketplace. This is the principal challenge faced in step 5 on the Process Improvement Road Map (Figure 14.1).

In the previous phases we focused on developing the structures and systems required to support process improvement and management. However, this work did not include the sociotechnical dimensions required to drive optimization. To enable optimization, we must impact our operating culture in significant ways. And that is not done by structures and systems alone.

SETTING THE PROCESS VISION

The ultimate process vision is to establish an operating culture that views continuous improvement as a natural and necessary component of organizational life and recognizes process as a key lever for sustaining and improving performance. In this vision, we have attained a self-sustaining state, where complex challenges are tackled by competent and intrinsically motivated employees at all levels. In this vision, improvement is a shared responsibility, where process improvement becomes a natural event that relies less on management push and more on self-directed employee pull. In this vision, employees are constantly driving waste and variation from our processes while at the same time they are making them more robust and adaptive.

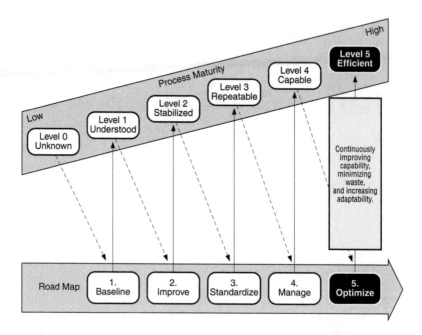

Figure 14.1 The Process Improvement Road Map for systematically advancing process maturity.

The process vision cannot be attained via directed activity, where senior managers initiate and manage improvement efforts via the traditional channels (for example, via systems of priorities and plans). Nor can it be attained by organizational leadership. It is only by making improvement relevant at the personal level that we can attain the self-sustaining state we are seeking.

At minimum, there are four key conditions to enabling the process vision. Here's a brief introduction to these conditions and specific approaches for fulfilling them:

• *Commitment.* The process vision requires that employees at all levels of the organization be intrinsically motivated to pursue continuous improvement. It's not enough to simply follow instructions; people must be personally engaged.

Dr. Peter Senge introduced a helpful concept, called *creative tension,* in *The Fifth Discipline.*[1] Creative tension describes the force that operates between current reality and a visionary state, and compels us toward the actions required to attain the visionary state. For creative tension to work, people must value the visionary state as personally important and be able to firmly hold the vision as they pursue closure of the gap. Failure to hold the vision will result in reduced effort; thereby reducing the likelihood the vision will be achieved.

The concept of creative tension can be instructive when we seek to use goals as a means to motivate people. The lesson to be learned is that the effectiveness of goals as motivators is related to the degree to which individuals hold them as personally relevant. Simply setting goals is insufficient. People must be personally invested in the goals before they can fuel creative tension.

• *Competency.* Employees must have the knowledge and skills required to be effective contributors to the process vision. To a large extent, the effectiveness of competency is determined by the degree of commitment present in individuals. In chapter 2 we discussed the need to grow organizational process competencies organically and incrementally. We sought to establish the basic competencies in phase 2 as we launched process improvement teams under the guidance of coaches. Now, we need to make it possible for employees to extend their process competencies as required (and just in time).

• *Clarity of purpose.* Employees must have a clear sense of what is important to the enterprise as well as the boundaries to self-directed effort. Although the process vision encourages self-directed effort, we want to ensure that effort is applied in ways that are beneficial to the needs of the enterprise. We must be aware that improvements in unimportant areas may represent poor investments of valuable enterprise resources. Clarity of purpose gives meaning to commitment and competency.

• *Opportunity.* Employees must have the opportunity to apply their competencies to improvement work as a natural part of their work life. It is important to note that the teaming process described in phase 3 can become a restraining force to the process vision if it is the only means for engaging people in process work. At this stage, we are seeking to clear the obstacles that impede the opportunity to engage in self-directed improvement work. Of course, opportunity must rest on the foundation elements of commitment, competency, and clarity of purpose to be utilized effectively.

ENABLING THE PROCESS VISION

Figure 14.2 outlines the high-level activities that are relevant to enabling the process vision. As with phase 7, these activities are not addressed just once, they must be addressed as a continuous cycle to sustain the vision.

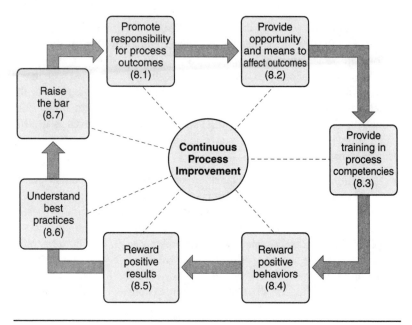

Figure 14.2 The activities in phase 8, Optimize Processes.

The following narrative provides additional clarification regarding theses activity areas.

8.1 PROMOTE RESPONSIBILITY FOR PROCESS OUTCOMES

As we discussed in Chapter 2, individual job goals are typically aligned with functional goals, not process goals. It is now time to resolve this disconnect by ensuring that individual job goals are designed and systematically measured in terms of their relationship to process goals. Jobs that contribute to multiple processes should include goals for each process supported. Since it is possible that process-related job goals might conflict with one another (within a job), it is important that we resolve potential conflicts before job goals are deployed. This can be accomplished by prioritizing process-level goals within jobs.

Although setting job goals that are aligned to process goals is a necessary first step, it is important to remember that the other enablers must be present to make job goal deployment meaningful. Without the other enablers, setting goals may only increase organizational stress.

8.2 PROVIDE OPPORTUNITY AND MEANS TO AFFECT OUTCOMES

Self-directed improvement does not mean that employees simply do whatever they wish. After all, we've taken great pains to establish the process ownership and management mechanisms required to preserve the integrity of process designs and execution practices. What it does mean is that employees should be able to freely initiate improvement proposals.

Catchball is a simple mechanism for enabling self-directed improvement. Using catchball, any person can initiate a potential improvement action by articulating a problem or opportunity along with proposed plans and then throwing them to other stakeholders for feedback and support. These communications can occur top-down or bottom-up. Either way, the approach enables a pull system of improvement.

As much as possible, employees initiating improvement recommendations should be afforded the opportunity to personally participate in, or even lead, the subsequent improvement activity. In cases where employees cannot create time for improvement work, the enterprise management should provide the relief required to enable participation. When we don't explicitly set the conditions that enable involvement, we are effectively disabling the process vision. Based on my experience, this is an area that is frequently overlooked as organizations deploy employee involvement programs.

8.3 PROVIDE TRAINING TO ENABLE GROWTH OF PROCESS COMPETENCIES

As processes grow in maturity (and capability) so do knowledge and skill requirements. For example, simple process improvement work has little need for statistical process control techniques, while process management does. Or, when we initially venture into measurement systems, we usually don't get involved in measurement repeatability and reproducibility issues. I'm frequently reminded of the expression "we don't know what we don't know" when trying to convince people there is more to learn. The failure to advance our understanding can, and frequently does, cause us to make significant errors in judgment. Earlier, we discussed the concept of tampering. Tampering is a classic example of making decisions that adversely impact process performance as a direct result of our efforts to improve performance.

Since we don't know what we don't know, it is important that we systematically push sufficient information to employees to make them aware that more advanced principles or tools are available. The purpose of this information is simply to fuel the tension required to establish employee pull. Educators tell us that adult learning occurs more effectively when there is a clearly perceived need. Simply pushing training to employees without the demand creation step ignores this factor. By balancing individual responsibility for improved results with the knowledge that higher-level tools are available, however, we establish the conditions necessary to fuel learning.

As a side note, we should mention that an additional benefit of the Process Improvement Road Map is that it helps us focus the learning that must occur as we advance the maturity of our processes. As we've moved through the previous phases, it should be clear that the knowledge and skill requirements changed significantly. For example, in the improve phase, we primarily needed to learn basic process improvement methods, in the standardize phase we needed to learn about documentation and control systems, and in the manage phase we needed to learn about measurement systems. To enable this progression, we must be prepared to teach the principles and techniques associated with each step.

8.4 REWARD POSITIVE BEHAVIOR

Most likely, the process vision implies significant cultural change to our organizations. Since culture involves how people think and believe, the common strategy for promoting cultural change involves trying to directly affect peoples thinking through various mechanisms like training, shared visioning, or motivational leadership. From my experience, however, this approach has a poor track record.

The science of behaviorism provides us with an alternative approach to change. Behaviorism postulates that since attitudes are largely unknowable, our efforts to impact them directly are generally ineffective or even counterproductive. Behaviorism also teaches us that not only can people's behavior be changed regardless of what their attitudes might be, once behavior has been changed, attitude usually follows.[2] Behaviorism provides us with the following principles:

- Behavior that is followed by a positive consequence (to the behaving individual) tends to repeat itself. This principle works if the consequence: (1) is to the behaving individual, (2) is positive, and (3) occurs soon after the action.

- Any consequence that occurs after an action and increases the frequency of that action is called a *positive reinforcer.*

- Behavior that is followed by a negative consequence or a painful event will decrease in frequency. However, there are problems with using negative consequences to manage behavior, including: (1) the person handing out the consequences often misinterprets what is, and what is not, a negative consequence, (2) they create unwanted side effects (people may become apprehensive), and (3) they may produce aggressive reactions.

The key lesson from these principles is that instead of directing our attention to decreasing the behaviors we don't want, we should direct our attention to increasing the behaviors we do want. In terms of translating these observations to strategy, we might want to take the following actions:

- Identify the behaviors that signal positive effort.

- Identify how we will detect those behaviors.

- Identify how we will provide positive consequences to those behaviors (keeping in mind that there are many potential responses that may be considered).

This process should be applied to all levels of the enterprise—from senior executives to frontline personnel.

8.5 REWARD POSITIVE RESULTS

Continuous improvement requires aspiration beyond the status quo. Actually, there must be a discomfort with the status quo that causes us to be on the lookout for improvement opportunities. Organizations frequently use annual goals as a means to fuel challenge. Self-directed improvement requires intrinsic motivation, however, which is not something that can be driven by an annual planning process alone.

A more effective strategy for driving aspiration is to reward positive results. By positive results, we're referring to meaningful outcomes that exceed the status quo. Recognized results can be planned (as part of a planning process) or unplanned (via self-directed action) so long as they make improvement personally relevant. Gain sharing provides a mechanism for allowing employees to share in the results of their collective efforts.

8.6 UNDERSTAND BEST PRACTICES

As we consider ways to improve process performance levels, we should begin looking both within and outside the enterprise for examples of performance levels and process designs that are worthy of emulation. Best practice information can be obtained from industry groups, professional associations and journals, consultants, and the Internet. It's a good idea to develop formal plans to structure this work. There is considerable information available to help us develop and execute effective best practices research efforts. The results from our best practices research can be leveraged in the following step to engage and challenge the process owners and process management teams.

8.7 RAISE THE BAR

Until now, we have primarily used process goals as a means for enabling process management (ensuring that our processes operate within acceptable ranges of behavior). Now, as we begin to consider improving process performance levels, we should consider ways to use process goals to guide and inspire action toward continuous improvement.

Of course, using goals is not as simple as simply passing predefined goals to employees and expecting action. Earlier, we talked about how the effectiveness of goals as motivators is related to the degree of personal relevance associated with them. This means that we need to develop ways to effectively invest employees in process goals. Although organizations frequently seek to invest employees by tying financial incentive to goals, my experience has shown this to be only a moderately effective approach. A more effective approach may be to involve employees in goal setting and goal management processes. In other words, raising the bar should become another behavioral component of the process vision.

15

Phase 9, Manage Program

As mentioned earlier, program management provides the leadership engine for the journey to process focus. In the initiate program phase (phase 2) we focused on establishing the structures and systems required to initiate program management. The manage program phase sustains that work by providing ongoing oversight and leadership for the process program.

In this phase the process council attends to the following ongoing responsibilities:

- Sets and deploys enterprise goals and strategies via core business processes.

- Manages program-level plans and accountabilities.

- Monitors priority process performance and related interventions.

- Sets and deploys enterprise budgets via core business processes.

- Maintains alignment between enterprise structures, systems, and core business processes.

- Leverages best practices across the enterprise.

The ultimate objective is that these responsibilities gradually become integrated into the fabric of enterprise management practices. That is, they become "the way we do things around here." We will discuss these responsibilities in greater detail in the following.

9.1 SET AND DEPLOY ENTERPRISE GOALS AND STRATEGIES VIA CORE PROCESSES

Enterprise Performance Goals and Strategies

Performance goals and enabling strategies are integral to effective enterprise performance management. It is therefore essential that senior management periodically reviews, revises, and restates enterprise performance goals and strategies as appropriate to reflect changing business conditions or priorities. Typically, this work is performed as part of the annual business planning cycle.

In a process-managed enterprise, it is also essential that business process goals be kept in alignment with enterprise goals and strategies. Therefore, as senior managers revise enterprise-level goals or strategies, those goals and strategies must be translated to the core business processes. The process council should communicate the new or revised process goals to the process owners. When setting process goals, the process council may want to revisit the steps outlined in phase 2, step 3.

Process owners are responsible for adjusting the process-level performance management systems as required to reflect new or revised process goals. Phase 3, step 3 describes the steps for translating goals into performance measurements.

9.2 MANAGE PROGRAM-LEVEL PLANS AND ACCOUNTABILITIES

In phase 2, the process council established process owners and process management teams to conduct the activities outlined in the process management and process improvement tracks of transformation strategy. The process council should maintain a system of status reporting and management reviews to assure that priority process work is progressing properly. The council must be vigilant in ensuring that deployment-related obstacles and performance issues are identified and resolved as quickly as possible. Since it is highly likely that problems will occur, failure to proactively identify and resolve them will simply allow the change initiative to deflate and lose momentum.

9.3 MONITOR PRIORITY PROCESS PERFORMANCE AND INTERVENTIONS

In phase 6, we instituted the process performance measurements required to manage process performance relative to the goals set by the process council (in phase 2). In phase 7, we established the measurements required to monitor process results and trends, and to drive corrective action interventions as required to realign performance. Process-level goals and performance metrics were also integrated into the enterprise performance dashboard to provide senior management with regular feedback regarding process performance and trends. These elements combine to provide an integrated system of process management that provides enterprise managers with the levers required to ensure nominal process performance as well as to direct improvement in performance capabilities.

To ensure the continued viability of the performance management, the process council should monitor process-level goal deployment, measurement systems, and improvement interventions. This can be accomplished by requiring regular updates from process owners and by performing periodic management reviews of process-level practices.

9.4 SET AND DEPLOY ENTERPRISE BUDGETS VIA CORE PROCESSES

As we discuss earlier, budget is the currency of the internal economy. Budget determines the levels and types of resources that are made available to perform work, as well as what projects will be funded to impact future capabilities. In a process-managed enterprise, resources and projects should be funded based on process needs, not just on the needs of disconnected departments.

Now is the time for enterprise managers to consider methods for transitioning from functionally derived budgets to process-derived budgets. By supporting our core processes as the first order of priority we are sending powerful messages throughout the enterprise and changing the basis by which funding requests are derived. Although budgets are determined by process, there is no reason why they cannot continue to be deployed and managed via traditional methods, that is, through the functional silos of the enterprise.

9.5 MAINTAIN ALIGNMENT BETWEEN STRUCTURES, SYSTEMS, AND PROCESSES

The process council is charged with ensuring alignment between key business processes and supporting organizational systems and structures. The council may assign individual members to take responsibility for certain organizational components or it may charter standing committees to fulfill this role.

Examples of the organizational structures and systems that require attention include strategy development and deployment, budgeting methods and systems, financial management systems, and human resource systems (including performance management, career models, and compensation and incentive systems). It is especially important that the systems that touch people and jobs be aligned with process performance and needs. Earlier, we discussed establishing job goals so as to reflect process goals and to link compensation increases to process performance. These simple changes will have a powerful impact on replacing the preeminence of the work unit (department) with the preeminence of process.

Process improvement proposals should explicitly consider organizational alignment issues and, where appropriate, include recommendations. The responsibility for implementing changes to organizational structures and systems should be made or approved by the process council.

9.6 MANAGE ENTERPRISE PERFORMANCE DASHBOARD

In phase 2, we positioned the enterprise performance dashboard as a key navigational system for enterprise management and as an enabler for the journey to process focus. The dashboard is where we sought to establish explicit linkages between business outcomes and business process performance. The dashboard gives enterprise managers new levers to pull when seeking to impact performance. Without these linkages, managers have no choice but to continue pulling the same levers as before.

Earlier, we suggested that the process council establish an ongoing responsibility for managing the operational aspects of the dashboard. These responsibilities may include oversight of data collection, storage, and analysis and reporting. The council must oversee this function to ensure that technical and operational aspects are handled satisfactorily. Moreover the council must take ownership for ensuring that enterprise goals are appropriately translated to the business processes as goals are added or revised.

9.7 LEVERAGE BEST PRACTICES

Best practices come into play in two ways. First, as process owners develop improved processing methods, there may be opportunities to leverage those methods in other business processes. These opportunities will not be readily visible from within the individual process areas. This puts the process council in the best position to determine the leveragability of best practices to other areas of the organization. When the process council is a council of process owners, this is a relatively straightforward assignment.

The second way best practices can come into play is when best practices are identified external to the organization. Regardless of who identifies a best practice, the process council is in the best position to determine the leveragability of practices across the enterprise.

9.8 INTEGRATE ADDITIONAL PROCESSES

In phase 2 we identified the priority processes that would be included in the initial transformation effort. As these processes are worked through the strategy, and capability and manageability issues firmly under control, the process council should consider including additional processes as appropriate. It is important to remember, of course, that we're talking about the relatively few value-creating business processes that comprise the enterprise, not the plethora of supporting or work processes.

9.9 COMMUNICATE VISION, PLANS, AND RESULTS

Continuous communication is a vital component of leadership. Communication is even more important when the organization is undertaking a significant change effort, like the journey to process focus. To this end, the process council should regularly reinforce the process vision and provide regular updates regarding program plans and results. This is also the time to acknowledge the efforts and accomplishments of program participants.

16

Closing

We have now completed our survey of the transformation strategy and its enabling tools. As mentioned in the preface, this strategy was conceived as a means for guiding the transformation of a functionally managed organization into a process-managed organization. In the preceding chapters we discussed how to establish the operating structures necessary to manage the relationships between enterprise goals, strategy, and business processes; to manage the alignment between enterprise structures, systems, and processes; and to manage enterprise performance via key business processes.

The strategy we covered offers a high-level view of the steps along the pathway to process focus. As a strategy, it does not try to cover the operational specifics that are normally included in a methodology. There is, to be sure, a great deal of planning and tool development required to execute the strategy. This detail planning provides practitioners with the opportunity and freedom to develop tools and techniques that offer the best organizational fit.

The strategy is not presented as the only way or the best way to attain process focus. It is, however, presented as the pathway designed by a real-world enterprise to guide its transformation effort. Earlier I mentioned that the strategy is built on a fairly integrated system of practices and structures. This means that, although adjustments will be required, and even encouraged, practitioners are cautioned to safeguard the overall integrity of the approach.

I like to view the strategy and supporting tools as living entities that are constantly evolving. This means that as we continue to learn more about what works or doesn't, or what works better, we continue to adjust the strategy to reflect our learning.

Process offers organizations a powerful lever for improving and managing performance. Before we can tap the full potential of this lever, however, we must expand our process paradigms to consider the highly interdependent relationships that exist between processes and organizational structures and systems. Many organizations believe that fixing process problems is the key to success. Hopefully, we've shown that this is an incomplete and ineffective strategy.

The transformation strategy and supporting tools we've covered in this book are offered as a guide to rethinking our process paradigms and charting a course that helps us more fully exploit the power of process.

Appendix A
Project Charter Template

PART 1, PROBLEM DEFINITION

1.1 Background

This section explains why the project is important *in business terms.* The background section should:

- Establish clear linkages between the process problem and business drivers, enterprise goals, or market requirements.

- Identify the business areas or dimensions that are being, or will be, impacted by the problem (for example, revenues, operating costs, service levels, market position, and so on.

- Establish quantified estimates of the project's potential impact along the business dimensions.

Example: Company X generates far more calls per customer per year than the other companies in the corporation or the industry norm. The greater number of calls has various impacts on the call center—including its ability to meet customer service levels and operating cost targets. Currently, company X experiences higher queue times and more blocked calls and has staffing levels 75 percent higher per customer than the industry norm or for other markets served by company X.

1.2 Problem Statement

The problem statement describes more specifically what is wrong with the process by identifying:

- The failure or shortfall in operational terms
- When and where the problem occurs
- The magnitude of the problem, in specific terms, if possible
- Who is impacted by the problem

The problem statement should describe an issue that is a known, verifiable, or measurable fact, and must not prejudge a root cause or contain a solution.

Example: The call index (calls/customer/year) for company X is believed to be 4.5, whereas the corporate call index is approximately 2.0 and the industry norm is 2.5.

1.3 Impacted Stakeholders

Identify the stakeholders who are impacted by the business problem as well as how they are impacted.

Example: Call center operations managers and customer service representatives are unable to meet service requirements, which impacts personal performance results. Customers are unable to reach customer service representatives and are indicating such on the customer satisfaction result. Repurchase patterns are trending unfavorably, possibly due to poor service levels.

1.4 Goal Statement

Goal statements are used to define success (that is, what is to be accomplished). Well-constructed goal statements are specific, measurable, attainable, relevant, and time bound (SMART) and are generally constructed using a three-part statement including: (1) a verb describing direction, (2) a process measure, and (3) a target value.

Example: Decrease company X's call index to 2.5 calls per customer per year by the end of 2002.

1.5 Priority and Dates

Identify the relative priority of the project and when completion is requested.

PART 2, PROJECT PLAN

2.1 Project Approach

Describe the organizational approach and methodology that will be used to conduct the project. Organizational approaches may vary in terms of team sizes and commitment levels. When describing methodology, be sure to note any tailoring that has been performed to the foundation methodology as well as any shortcuts that are anticipated.

2.2 Project Organization

Identify the roles and occupants that will participate in the project. It is essential to explicitly define the amount of time the various roles are expected to contribute to the project and who will ensure this time is made available. Generally, time contributions are expressed as a full-time employee (FTE) percentage.

1. Project champion—identify the person who will champion the project and team.

2. Team coach—identify individual who will facilitate and lead the team.

3. Team members—identify the core team members.

4. Supporting cast—identify the subject matter experts (SMEs) who will be made available to support the team.

2.3 Project Scope

Defining project scope is essential to ensure that process improvement teams work within the appropriate solution space. The scope statement should identify:

- What processes the team should focus on

- The boundaries of those processes

- What (if anything) is out of bounds for the team

Example: The team will focus on the call-handling process for company X, including all types of calls. Initially, the team will determine which call types represent the greatest improvement potential. When the field is narrowed to the vital few (by applying the 80/20 rule), the team will need to determine if there are ways to align company X's call volume with industry averages. Technology-based solutions are outside the scope of this effort.

2.4 Project Work Plan

Describe the work breakdown structure for the project.

2.5 Project Deliverables and Dates

Identify key project milestones and deliverables and establish target dates for completion of these milestones and deliverables. Milestones may include process steps (for example, DMAIC) or delivery of work products (for example, deployment plan, training, or documentation).

Example: The team will have the analysis phase of work completed by July 1, 2002. Implementation dates will be dependent on major process and system changes, which will be addressed in the improvement proposal.

Milestones and due dates include:

1. Prepare project proposal by mm/dd/yy.

2. Conduct project chartering by mm/dd/yy.

3. Approve the charter by mm/dd/yy.

2.6 Project Budget

If appropriate, describe the nonpersonnel resources that will be made available to the team (including space, budget, training, supplies, and people). Be sure to include any decision limits and reporting requirements that may be imposed on the project team. In many cases, this section may be optional.

2.7 Constraints, Assumptions, and Risks

This section should describe any constraints the project team will face, any major assumptions the project team is making, or any concerns that need to be addressed during the project.

PART 3, PROJECT COMPLETION REPORT

Part 3 is completed at project conclusion to record results, identify continuing plans and responsibilities, and record lessons learned.

3.1 Project Completion Summary

Describe how the project was concluded—including what goals were attained or not attained.

3.2 Projected Results

Identify the savings projected to be delivered by the project.

Hard Savings. Hard dollar savings are monetary savings from the elimination of company costs as a result of the process improvement. Examples include the elimination of FTEs and the associated costs including payroll, 401K and ATPI benefits, and other costs attributable to the position (training, travel, and so on). Also includes elimination of temporary staff or other contracted services.

Soft Savings. Soft savings are potential monetary savings from freeing-up capacity. Examples include elimination of partial FTEs to perform other tasks. Value of savings includes percentage of 401K, ATPI benefits, and other costs attributable to the capacity gains.

Intangible Savings. Include other desired outcomes as a result of process improvement. Includes improvements in customer satisfaction, reductions in process cycle time, and creation of market advantage.

3.3 Deployment Plan

Describe how project deployment was/will be handled—including key steps, dates, and responsibilities.

3.4 Savings Ownership

Indicate who has primary responsibility for ensuring the gains provided by the project are indeed realized. This includes making the management decisions required to take hard savings and for ensuring that the capacity freed by soft savings is effectively utilized.

3.5 Review Plan

Describe when and how the postimplementation review will be conducted. Be sure to identify who has responsibility for planning and conducting the review.

3.6 Lessons Learned

Describe key lessons learned from the project that may benefit other projects or the organization as a whole.

PART 4,
POSTIMPLEMENTATION REVIEW

Part 4 is completed during the postimplementation review to assess implementation effectiveness and actual results delivered.

4.1 Measured Results

Identify the hard savings, soft savings, and intangible savings measured during the postimplementation review.

4.2 Other Findings

Describe other relevant findings resulting from the postimplementation review.

PART 5, REVISION RECORD

Create the revision record.

Revision/Date	Description
Rev 1—mm/dd/yyyy	Initial draft of project team charter.

Appendix B

Process Improvement Audit Checklist

Process: Audit Date:

Audit Criteria	Meets Criteria	Comments
1. *Customer Perceptions*		
☐ Are process customers aware the process has been changed?		
☐ Are process customers aware of the targeted improvement objectives?		
☐ Have customers been surveyed or polled to determine if the changes have yielded targeted improvements?		
☐ Have customers noticed any changes in the usability or performance of the process? What are they?		
☐ Do customers understand how to communicate performance feedback? Have they provided feedback regarding any/all negative experiences?		
☐ Has the change impacted customer perception of the process in any way?		

continued

Audit Criteria	Meets Criteria	Comments
2. *Deployment*		
☐ Is there a documented deployment plan?		
(List the action items defined in the deployment plan and validate that each was satisfactorily completed.)		
☐ _____		
☐ _____		
☐ _____		
☐ _____		
☐ _____		
3. *Compliance*		
☐ Do employees understand the process and do they posses the skills necessary to execute the process?		
☐ Are operating procedures being followed consistently and accurately? *(Formulate five to 10 validation questions based on operational documentation and include them below.)*		
1. For example, Are control totals being tallied and recorded in control logs as described in the process documentation?		
2. For example, Are customer requests being reviewed by CSR to ensure completion and accuracy before routing to new business representative?		
☐ Are operating reports being generated on schedule, completely, and accurately?		
☐ Are process performance measurements being collected properly?		
☐ Are exceptions handled in accordance with process policy?		

continued

Audit Criteria	Meets Criteria	Comments
4. *Managed*		
☐ Is there a process owner established and does the owner understand and practice the role?		
☐ Does the process owner regularly review process performance data and take corrective actions as appropriate?		
☐ Does the process owner activity solicit feedback and improvement ideas from employees?		
☐ Is there a system of controls in place to ensure that line managers are aware of the degree and effectiveness of compliance to process standards?		
☐ Do line managers effectively utilize the system of controls?		
☐ Have line managers made corrections to align operating practices to process standards?		
☐ Have employees received any feedback regarding process performance or corrective action needs?		
☐ Have employees provided any feedback regarding process performance or improvement ideas?		
5. *Results*		
List key performance metrics below and indicate any favorable or unfavorable results or trends for each.		
☐ _____		
☐ _____		
☐ _____		

continued

continued

Audit Criteria	Meets Criteria	Comments
6. *Improvements* ☐ Do customers or employees have any improvement suggestions regarding the process or its deployment?		

Audit Team

_____   _____

_____   _____

Signatures:

Process owner: _____ Date: _____

Team leader: _____ Date: _____

Auditor: _____ Date: _____

Appendix C

Process and Quality Management System Manual Template

CONTENTS

–i–

PREFACE

This document describes the process and quality management system used by *[company name]* to manage the *[process name]*. The system is based on the five-level architecture described in Figure C.1. These levels are briefly described below.

Process management. Process management serves as the foundation for the system by defining the operating practices and accountabilities used to guide execution of the five process components shown in Figure C.1 (that is, inputs, methods, equipment, environment, and personnel). By establishing clear practices and accountabilities for each component, process management promotes accurate and repeatable execution of processes.

Process control. Whereas process management establishes standards for process execution, process control monitors the performance characteristics of key process components to ensure they continue to perform appropriately. The key elements in process control are goals, measures, and control plans.

Quality control. Quality control ensures that only quality products are released to customers. Traditionally, this involves the use of statistically relevant sampling to determine output quality levels and control plans to govern the disposition of products prior to release. Measured quality levels may be communicated to customers as a way to certify quality levels.

Customer acceptance. Customer acceptance describes how customers determine the suitability of incoming product or services. Acceptance practices may range from incoming inspection to the use of certifications. Customer acceptance and quality control practices must be maintained in alignment at all times.

System quality assurance. System QA ensures that the overall process and quality management system continues to function effectively by monitoring internal work products and practices, statistical analysis of internal measurements, and management reviews.

All five levels are connected to a system of continuous process improvement to identify and resolve root causes of operational deficiencies and to continuously improve process capability.

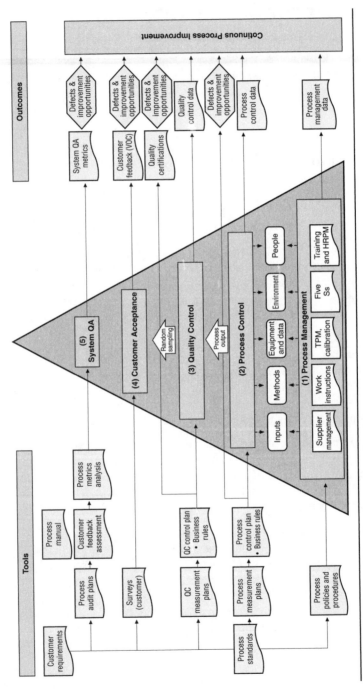

Figure C.1 Process and quality management system.

PROCESS OVERVIEW

Introduce the process by describing its purpose and relationship to the enterprise it supports. Describe the key outcomes of the process and how those outcomes contribute to enterprise performance. Position the process relative to organizational structures (that is, what organizational components participate in the process) and the other processes operating within the enterprise (that is, what are the key process interdependencies).

0.1 Process Scope

Include a narrative description of the process scope. The purpose of scope is to provide a clear definition of the process boundaries (clarifying what's in and what's outside the process) and the process drivers (the things that cause the process to respond).

0.2 Process Model

Include a high-level process map to describe the process boundaries, interfaces, and content. A SIPOC diagram provides the appropriate information.

0.3 Customers, Outputs, and Exit Requirements

Describe the key customers of the process. Customers are the people and organizations that receive the outputs of the process. For each customer, identify the products and services it receives from the process. Customer requirements for each product and service will be further defined in section 3.2.1.

0.4 Suppliers, Inputs, and Entry Requirements

Describe the key suppliers of the process. Suppliers are the people and organizations that provide inputs to the process. For each supplier, identify the major inputs it supplies to the process. Quality requirements for each input will be defined in section 1.1.2.

0.5 Process Ownership

Identify who has ownership responsibility for the process design and supporting documentation and tools.

0.6 Process Change Management

Summarize the key policies and methods used to assure that process changes are proposed, developed, and deployed in a controlled manner.

1. PROCESS MANAGEMENT

Process management establishes the operational standards required to manage the key components of processes. Brief descriptions of each follow.

Inputs. When process performance is dependent on the quality of its inputs, it is appropriate to establish standard practices for proactively managing inputs. Input management practices are generally established as part of a supplier management program.

Methods. Process designs are translated into work methods to enable repeatable execution of designs. Methods describe how we conduct process work. The primary tools used to enable standard work methods include policies and procedures, work instructions, templates, and checklists.

Equipment and data. Frequently, processes incorporate various types of equipment (ranging from simple hand tools to sophisticated technology) and data. When processes are highly dependent on equipment and data, it is appropriate to establish programs designed to ensure their continued reliability and availability. Commonly used approaches to managing equipment include calibration, preventive maintenance, backup, and disaster recovery.

Environment. Processes operate in environments. Environmental factors may include facilities, working arrangements, and ambient conditions. To the degree that environmental factors are relevant to process performance, it is appropriate to describe how they are to be managed.

Personnel. Since processes use people to execute the methods and operate the equipment, it is appropriate to define how skills are going to be developed and maintained in order to sustain effective process performance. Commonly used approaches include new employee training, performance assessments, incentives, and certification programs.

1.1 Inputs

Input management focuses on ensuring that incoming work products meet process entry standards. Several methods may be used, including incoming inspection, upstream audits, and supplier quality systems. Although supplier quality systems are the preferred method, incoming inspection and upstream audits may be warranted, depending on the demonstrated capability of supplier production and quality systems.

1.1.1 Input Requirements

Identify the inputs used by the process. This includes process initiators (orders) and raw materials that are consumed by the process. Input material requirements are generally expressed as attributes and service requirements as behaviors. Each attribute or behavior should be defined in terms that are measurable and include the appropriate acceptance standards.

1.1.2 Incoming Inspection

If incoming inspection is used, the following items should be completed.

   a. Incoming inspection policy. *State the incoming inspection policy for the process. The policy describes the scope and nature of incoming inspection and sets the key accountabilities associated with managing and performing inspection.*

   b. Incoming product quality characteristics. *Identify the product and service requirements that will be evaluated via incoming inspection.*

   c. Sampling and measurement. *Describe the sampling and measurement methods that are used to assess the incoming quality level. The sampling methods and measurement methods outlined in this section must be reflected in the appropriate operating procedures in section x.*

   d. Supplier corrective action system. *Describe the system for reporting and resolving quality problems identified via incoming inspection. The suppler corrective action system requires that suppliers identify and resolve the root causes of quality problems. The system description must identify how problems are reported and tracked.*

e. Records and reporting. *Describe the records and data elements that will be maintained as the basis for evaluating supplier quality performance and driving supplier continuous improvement.*

1.1.3 Supplier Management

a. *Supplier audits.* Supplier audits may be used to determine and/or validate the maturity of supplier quality systems and process capabilities. If audits are used, they should be described in this section.

b. *Supplier quality systems.* Supplier quality systems assure the delivery of conforming material and information to the process. To the degree that suppliers are able to demonstrate capable and mature quality systems, incoming inspection and supplier audits can be eliminated or minimized. In this section we describe our policies and expectations regarding supplier quality systems.

c. *Supplier continuous improvement.* The ability to continuously improve the value delivered to customers depends, in part, on the ability of suppliers to improve delivered value as well. In this section we describe our policies and expectations regarding supplier continuous improvement. It is appropriate to describe continuous improvement targets and time frames, the methods that may be used as the basis for improvement work and the key accountabilities associated with improvement.

1.2 Methods

Process designs are translated into work methods to enable accurate and repeatable execution of designs. These work methods are documented via standard operating policies and procedures, work instructions, and supporting tools. The job responsibility matrix identifies the procedural responsibilities by job. The resource inventory identifies the personnel available to perform process work, job

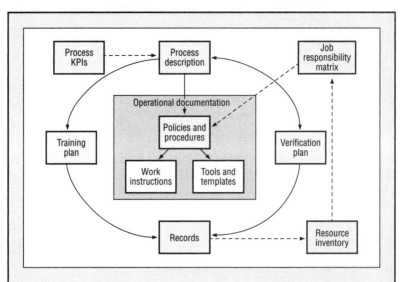

Figure C.2   PQMS documentation system.

qualifications, and current job assignments. The training plan describes when and how personnel are trained in process methods and tools, and the verification plan describes when and how compliance to methods is verified. Records are maintained for training and verification activities. Figure C.2 describes how these elements combine to support the methods component.

1.2.1 Policies and Procedures Index

Policies and procedures describe operating policies and who does what, while work instructions describe how procedures are performed. Work instructions are generally used when detailed instructions are required to conduct a task.

Include a list of the operating procedures with navigational links.

1.2.2 Work Instructions Index

Work instructions describe precisely how a method is to be performed. Examples of work instructions might include how to calibrate a machine or how to recover from an exception condition. Work instructions may link to numerous policies and procedures.

Include a list of the work instructions with navigational links.

1.2.3 Forms and Templates Index

Forms and templates facilitate execution of procedures and work instructions.

Include a list of the templates used in executing process work with navigational links.

1.2.4 Job Responsibility Matrix

The job responsibility matrix identifies operational procedure responsibilities by job. A job is a role that may be occupied by one or more people and will generally be associated with multiple operating procedures. Each procedure that is associated with a job is assigned one of the following codes to indicate the nature of the responsibility:

(R) to indicate the job is responsible for performing the procedure.

(A) to indicate the job is responsible for ensuring the procedure is performed properly.

(I) to indicates the job is responsible for staying informed regarding performance of the procedure.

The responsibility for the content of operating procedures is defined in the procedures themselves. In section 1.4.1 we will identify the personnel resources available to perform process work and their job qualifications and assignments.

Include a link to the job responsibility matrix.

1.2.5 Training Plan and Records

The training plan describes how and how often skills will be assessed, and how skills are developed.

Include a link to the training plan.

1.2.6 Verification Plan and Records

The verification plan describes how and how often compliance to procedures and instructions is verified, and how verification results are used to drive corrective action.

Include a link to the training plan.

1.3 Equipment and Data

In this section we describe the process management practices for equipment and data. First, we identify the equipment and data that are managed as part of the process and quality management system. Then, we describe how calibration, preventive maintenance, and backup methods are used to ensure their continued reliability and availability.

1.3.1 Equipment and Data Inventory

The equipment and data inventory may be maintained externally from this manual as part of the resource inventory.

Include a link to the equipment and data inventory.

1.3.2 Calibration Programs

Equipment calibration programs may be used to ensure effective operating performance of certain types of equipment. If calibration programs are used, they should be described in this section along with linkages to the supporting policies and procedures. The program descriptions should include lists of the equipment that is included. Calibration policies and procedures should also be listed in section 1.2.1.

Include a list of the calibration programs with navigational links to supporting policies and procedures.

1.3.3 Preventive Maintenance Programs

Preventive maintenance programs may be used to ensure continued operation of equipment. If preventive maintenance programs are used, they should be described in this section along with links to the supporting policies and procedures. The program descriptions should include lists of the equipment that are included. Preventive maintenance policies and procedures should also be listed in section 1.2.1.

Include a list of the preventive maintenance programs with navigational links to supporting policies and procedures.

1.3.4 Backup Programs

Backup programs may be used to ensure continued availability of equipment and data. If backup programs are used, they should be described in this section along with linkages to the supporting policies and procedures. The program descriptions should include lists of the equipment and records that are included. Backup policies and procedures should also be listed in section 1.2.1.

Include a list of the backup programs with navigational links to supporting policies and procedures.

1.4 Environment

In this section we describe the process management practices for key environmental factors. Managed characteristics might include individual work space (sufficiency and organization), common work spaces (pathways, shared spaces), ergonomics (seating) and ambient conditions (temperature, noise, and lighting). Related policies and procedures should be documented in the methods section.

1.4.1 Environmental Factors Inventory

Identify the environmental factors that are managed via the process quality management system (PQMS). Operating policies and procedures should be prepared to define specific accountabilities for each factor and assigned to jobs via the job responsibility matrix.

1.5 Personnel

In this section we describe the process management practices for people. Generally, these practices include: (1) inventorying personnel, (2) assessing personnel skill levels relative to standards (where standards are set via procedures and work instructions), and (3) developing skills as required to attain standards.

1.5.1 Personnel Inventory

The personnel inventory identifies the resources available to perform process work. For each resource, we identify the job qualifications (via procedure-level certifications) and current job assignments. By indicating which procedures a resource is qualified to perform, we enable more effective alignment between job skills and assignments. The personnel inventory may be maintained externally from this manual as part of the resource inventory.

Include a link to the personnel inventory.

1.5.2 Skills Assessments

Describe the methods used to assess the skill levels of the occupants of the jobs identified in the job responsibility matrix. Skill assessments provide the basis for certifying job skills and for identifying developmental needs by assuring occupants have the knowledge and skills required to perform the procedures associated with their jobs.

Include a list of the jobs that will be assessed under the skills assessment program and indicate the assessment methods that will be utilized for each.

1.5.3 Skills Development

Describe the methods used to develop and reinforce process-related skills. Include a list of the process roles covered by the skill development program and indicate the methods that will be used for each. It is not necessary or appropriate to include curriculum or training materials in this document as they will be documented separately.

2. PROCESS CONTROL

Whereas process management establishes standards for process execution, process control monitors the performance characteristics of key process components to ensure they are performing appropriately. Process control seeks to determine process outcomes by proactively managing the internal determinants of outcomes using quantitative methods.

2.1 Process Control Standards

Process control standards describe the desired outcomes or behaviors for each of the five process components. Generally, standards are expressed as physical characteristics when dealing with physical work products and as behaviors when dealing with services. Control standards are not quality standards. Rather, they are the internal standards used to manage individual process components in order to ensure that process-level outputs meet customer requirements (quality).

It is helpful to define control standards as desired outcomes (as end states) before getting into measurement issues. Examples may include: inputs are received on time, equipment is available 99 percent, or people possess required skills. Of course, these end states must correlate favorably to process quality or they have little predictive value.

Identify the process control standards that are used to gauge the performance of the five process components.

2.2 Process Control Measurements

Process control measurements translate standards into measurable phenomena. The goal–question–metric (GQM) technique provides a straightforward method for developing measurements based on goals.

The informational value of measurements can be greatly increased when they are normalized. Generally, this involves expressing them as ratios or multiples (for example, calls processed within standard/total number of calls processed).

Process control measurements should be recorded as time series data to enable the types of analysis required to know when corrective actions are warranted. Process control practices must avoid the temptation to tamper with processes.

Identify the process control measurements that are used to monitor performance relative to the process control standards.

2.3 Process Control Plans

Process control involves action. To enable appropriate actions, we must describe, in advance, the actions we will take when certain out-of-control conditions exist. We describe these actions in process control plans.

List the process control plans that are being used to practice process control.

2.4 Process Improvement Practices

Poor process performance warrants systematic investigation and possible adjustments to processes. Here we describe our practices for initiating process improvement work based on unfavorable process performance results.

Describe the policy for initiating process improvement efforts based on process performance results.

3. QUALITY CONTROL

Quality control (QC) ensures that only quality products are released to customers. QC utilizes postprocess sampling and inspection to assess quality levels of products and services. Sample groups failing to meet acceptable quality levels are corrected and reevaluated before release to the customer. Nonconformances are forwarded to the corrective action system to identify and resolve root causes.

3.1 Quality Control Policy

Here we state the QC policy for the process. The policy should describe the scope and nature of postprocess inspection, the key accountabilities associated with managing and performing product inspection and the disposition of nonconforming work products. The policy must align with customer quality control and acceptance requirements.

State the QC policy.

3.2 Quality Control Standards

3.2.1 Customer Quality Requirements

Identify the product and/or service characteristics that are used by customers to determine the quality of the products and services they receive from the process. Generally, product quality is translated into product attributes and service quality into services behaviors. For each attribute or behavior, describe the acceptable quality levels (AQL) and the methods customers will use for assessing delivered quality. Customer quality requirements are to be described from the customer's perspective and in customer terms.

List the customer quality requirements.

3.2.2 Quality Control Specifications

Customer requirements may require translation into our terminology, measures, and acceptance standards. In this section, we describe the quality attributes and specifications that will be validated via QC practices. Theses are the criteria that are used as the basis for approving products and services before release to customers. When translation is necessary, it is essential that we map our specifications to customer requirements to provide traceability.

List the quality control specifications.

3.3 Quality Control Measurements

3.3.1 QC Measurement Definitions

Product control specifications are translated into measurement terms that are expressed via normalized metrics and recorded as time-series data.

Describe the measurements and supporting metrics that will be used to monitor process quality.

3.3.2 QC Sampling and Measurement

Describe the sampling and measurement methods that are used to assess the quality level of work products and services. The sampling methods and measurement methods outlined in this section must be reflected in the appropriate operating procedures in section 1.2.1.

3.3.3 QC Records and Reporting

Describe the records and data elements that will be maintained as the basis for substantiating product quality and to support continuous improvement activities.

3.4 Quality Control Practices

3.4.1 Quality Control Plans

Since the purpose of QC is to ensure that only suitable products are released to customers, we must describe, in advance, the actions that will be taken when undesirable outcomes are detected. These actions are described in quality control plans.

List the quality control plans that are being used to practice quality control. Control plans may be documented as tools that are associated with operating policies and procedures.

3.4.2 Corrective Action System

Corrective action systems focus on identifying and resolving the root causes to quality problems identified via quality control.

Describe the system for reporting and resolving quality problems identified via product QC. The system description must identify how problems are reported, tracked, and resolved as well as how solutions are deployed and controlled. Identify the operating policies and procedures that support this system.

3.5 Quality Improvement Practices

Poor quality performance warrants systematic investigation and possible adjustments to processes. Here we describe our practices for initiating process improvement work based on unfavorable quality performance results.

Describe the policy for initiating process improvement efforts based on quality performance results.

4. CUSTOMER QUALITY ACCEPTANCE

Since the overarching purpose of the PQMS is to ensure that process outcomes consistently meet customer expectations, it is essential that our system be effectively linked to our customers' systems to ensure continued alignment and for collecting regular performance feedback. We accomplish these tasks by: (1) keeping abreast of customer requirements, (2) aligning our QC system to the customer's system of acceptance, and (3) driving regular feedback from customers.

4.1 Customer Requirement Reviews

Customer requirements reviews are positioned as the primary mechanism for ensuring continued and accurate understanding of customer requirements. By using a formal approach to periodically validating requirements, we avoid the risks associated with requirements creep. Once customer requirements are baselined, this should be the only means by which they are revised.

Describe the customer requirements review program.

4.2 Customer Acceptance Methods

Customers have a variety of choices for ensuring the acceptability of incoming products or services—including, mostly, common incoming inspection and certificates of quality. When customers rely on incoming inspection, our QC measurements and standards should be aligned with their inspection practices and criteria. The use of certificates of quality reduces the need for incoming inspection, but requires higher levels of customer confidence.

Describe customer acceptance methods and criteria.

4.3 Customer Feedback

Without systematic feedback from customers it is impossible to clearly know perceptions regarding performance levels. Generally, feedback should be solicited at two levels: (1) quantitative feedback regarding tangibles (factors that can be measured) and (2) qualitative feedback regarding intangible factors (perceptions and satisfaction responses).

Describe the methods for soliciting customer feedback.

5. SYSTEM QUALITY ASSURANCE

System quality assurance monitors internal process quality by monitoring internal work products and practices. The primary tools used to support system QA include system auditing, customer feedback assessment, metrics analysis, and management reviews.

5.1 System Auditing

5.1.1 Audit Schedule and Methods

Describe the schedule and methods for conducting system audits. Auditing procedures should be documented via standard policies and procedures.

5.1.2 Escalation Procedure

Describe the procedure for handling nonconformances detected via system audits. The policy should describe the conditions that warrant escalation, as well as the types of escalations that may be appropriate. Escalation procedures should be documented via standard polices and procedures.

5.1.3 Records and Reporting

Describe the records and data elements that will be maintained as the basis for substantiating audit findings.

5.2 Customer Feedback Assessment

Describe the schedule, methods, and accountabilities for evaluating customer feedback.

5.3 Process Metrics Analysis

Describe the schedule, methods, and accountabilities for evaluating process control and quality control metrics.

5.4 Management Reviews

Management reviews are used to regularly and systematically update enterprise management regarding process and quality performance. The information covered during the reviews should include: (1) customer feedback, (2) quality control and process control data analysis, (3) supplier performance, and (4) system audit results. These reviews may result in setting improvement targets and/or dispatching corrective actions.

Management reviews should also be conducted with customers on a regular basis to ensure continued alignment regarding expectations, delivered results and future plans.

Describe the schedule, methods, and accountabilities for conducting management reviews.

6. CONTINUOUS PROCESS IMPROVEMENT SYSTEM

6.1 Receiving, Prioritizing, and Tracking Issues

Describe how issues are received and tracked. Procedures should be defined and deployed to establish clear responsibility for issue receipt, management, and tracking.

6.2 Planning and Managing Improvement Work

Process improvement work is frequently conducted as team-based project work. Using teams to engage employees who have first-hand knowledge of process operations has the potential to produce higher-quality solutions and more effective solution deployments. However, to translate this potential into reality, teams must be sufficiently skilled and well managed.

Process improvement team members should have a good understanding of improvement methods and tools before they become engaged in process work. Without reasonable skill levels, work quality will suffer and much of our time will be consumed in coaching individuals and performing rework. Therefore, it is a good idea to incorporate the process improvement training as part of the

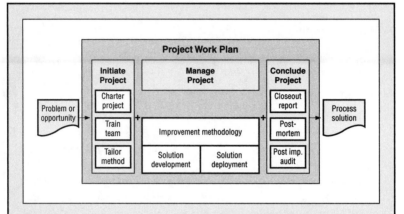

Figure C.3   Process improvement project management process.

project launch process. Of course, employees already trained may skip this step.

Good project management practices are also integral to successful process improvement projects. If projects are poorly planned, managed, or concluded, it is unlikely that they will produce the solutions we desire in a timely manner. Figure C.3 shows how project management practices can be combined with training and methodology to enable effective management of the end-to-end projects. This project management process utilizes three stages to initiate, manage, and conclude projects.

6.2.1 Initiate Projects

Project initiation begins with a presenting problem or opportunity and concludes with a trained and chartered project team. This is where we evaluate the issue, determine the impacted stakeholders, identify and/or tailor the improvement methodology to meet project needs, set the project team and conduct required training, and prepare the initial project charter. These steps are essential to getting a good start and maintaining clear focus throughout the project.

Describe the approach used to initiate improvement projects.

6.2.2 Manage Projects

The manage project stage begins with the charter and methodology from the define project phase and concludes with a validated and deployed solution. Progress relative to the plan should be monitored and reported to sponsoring management on a regular basis. Sponsoring managers are encouraged to actively monitor progress and to occasionally attend project activities to provide support as required.

Describe how projects are managed, while paying particular attention to managing project plans and regularly reporting status to key stakeholders.

6.2.3 Conclude Projects

This is where we perform the activities required to successfully conclude projects and to ensure that the appropriate organizational learning occurs. This stage should also include a postimplementation audit to ensure that the improvements were effectively assimilated by the organization and that they are delivering expected results.

Describe how projects are concluded, while paying particular attention to closeout reporting and follow-up activities.

Appendix D
Process Control Plan

Process Name:

Process Owner:

Page		of	
Rev #		Rev Date:	mm/dd/yy

Process Steps / Location (flowchart)

Department A — Control Ck No

- Receive incoming order → Validate Enter customer no. → Customer no. error?
  - Yes → Return order
  - No → Scan order form (11) → Transmit image to OCR department

Department B

- OCR reads image (12) → Determine correction requirements → Manual required?
  - Yes → Manual posting
  - No → Auto posting → Transmit orders (13) → p2

Ck No	Who Checks	When to Check	Where to Check	What to Check	Metric No	Target LSL	Target USL	Response Plan
				— *Examples* —				
11	Scanner operator	Every 10th order	Customer name on image	Image quality	23	Legible	None	If name not legible, stop and clean scanner. Rescan orders since last check.
12	OCR system	10% random sample	Customer name and address fields	Character read rate	31	98.5%	None	Recalibrate color shift.
13	Network operator	Every hour on the hour	Transmit log	Transmit time	68	None	30 sec	Reset communication lines.

Endnotes

Preface

1. Dirk Dusharme, "Survey: Six Sigma Packs a Punch," *Quality Digest* 23, no. 11 (November 2003): 24.
2. Michael Hammer, *The Agenda* (New York: Crown Business, 2001).

Chapter 1

1. Michael Beer, "Why Total Quality Management Programs Do Not Persist," *Decision Sciences* 34, no. 4 (2003): 623.
2. Peter Keen, *The Process Edge: Creating Value Where It Counts* (Cambridge, MA: Harvard Business School Press, 1997).
3. Kevin B. Hendricks and Vinod Singhal, "Does Implementing an Effective TQM Program Actually Improve Operating Performance?" *Management Science* 43 (September 1997): 1258–74; Kevin B. Hendricks and Vinod Singhal, "The Long-Run Stock Price Performance of Firms with Effective TQM Programs," *Management Science* 47 (March 2001): 359–68.
4. Geary A. Rummler and Alan P. Brache, *Improving Performance: How to Manage the White Space on the Organization Chart* (San Francisco: Jossey-Bass, 1995).
5. Stephen Covey, *The Seven Habits of Highly Effective People* (New York: Simon & Schuster, 1990).
6. Frederick F. Reichheld, *The Loyalty Effect: The Hidden Force Behind Growth, Profits, and Lasting Value* (Boston: Bain and Company, 1996).
7. Bradley T. Gale, *Managing Customer Value: Creating Quality and Service That Customers Can See* (New York: Free Press, 1994).

8. Robert B. Woodruff and Sarah Gardial, *Know Your Customer: New Approaches to Understanding Customer Value and Satisfaction* (Malden, MA: Blackwell Publishers, 1996).

9. Robert Gardner, "What Do Customers Value?" *Quality Progress* 34, no. 11 (November 2001): 41–48.

10. Eliyahu M. Goldratt, *Theory of Constraints* (Great Barrington, MA: North River Press, 1990).

11. See note 3 above.

12. Ibid.

Chapter 2

1. Eliyahu M. Goldratt, *Theory of Constraints* (Great Barrington, MA: North River Press, 1990).

2. Peter Keen, *The Process Edge: Creating Value Where It Counts* (Cambridge, MA: Harvard Business School Press, 1997).

3. Geary A. Rummler and Alan P. Brache, *Improving Performance: How to Manage the White Space on the Organization Chart* (San Francisco: Jossey-Bass, 1995).

4. See note 1 above.

5. Stephen Covey, *The Seven Habits of Highly Effective People* (New York: Simon & Schuster, 1990).

6. Robert Gardner, "Ten Process Improvement Lessons for Leaders," *Quality Progress* 35 (November 2002): 56–61.

7. Elizabeth K. Keating, Rogelio Oliva, Nelson P. Repenning, Scott Rockart, and John D. Sterman, "Overcoming the Improvement Paradox," *European Management Journal* 17, no. 2: 120–34.

8. Michael Beer, Russell Eisenstat, and Bert Spector, "Why Change Programs Don't Produce Change," *Harvard Business Review* 68, no. 6 (November–December 1990): 158–66.

9. See note 7 above.

10. Robert Gardner, "Resolving the Process Paradox," *Quality Progress* 34 (March 2001): 51–59.

11. Arthur M. Schneiderman, "Setting Quality Goals: Use Observed Rates of Continuous Improvement to Position Targets," *Quality Progress* 21, no. 4 (April 1988): 51.

12. See note 7 above.

Chapter 3

1. Michael Hammer, *The Agenda* (New York: Crown Business, 2001).

2. Gabriel A. Pall, *The Process Centered Enterprise: The Power of Commitments* (Boca Raton, FL: St. Lucie Press, 2000).

3. Bill Wortman, *CQM Primer* (West Terre Haute, IN: Quality Council of Indiana, 1996).

Chapter 4

1. Michael Hammer, *The Agenda* (New York: Crown Business, 2001).
2. See note 1 above.
3. Geary A. Rummler and Alan P. Brache, *Improving Performance: How to Manage the White Space on the Organization Chart* (San Francisco: Jossey-Bass, 1995).
4. Eliyahu M. Goldratt, *Theory of Constraints* (Great Barrington, MA: North River Press, 1990).

Part II

1. Dirk Dusharme, "Survey: Six Sigma Packs a Punch," *Quality Digest* 23, no. 11 (November 2003): 24.

Chapter 7

1. Robert S. Kaplan and David P. Norton, *The Balanced Scorecard: Translating Strategy into Action* (Cambridge, MA: Harvard Business School Press, 1996).
2. Michael Hammer, course material.

Chapter 8

1. Robert S. Kaplan and David P. Norton, *The Balanced Scorecard: Translating Strategy into Action* (Cambridge, MA: Harvard Business School Press, 1996).

Chapter 9

1. Michael L. George, *Lean Six Sigma* (New York: McGraw Hill, 2002).

Chapter 14

1. Peter M. Senge, *The Fifth Discipline: The Art and Science of the Learning Organization* (New York: Doubleday Currency, 1990).
2. Ferdinand F. Fournies, *Coaching For Improved Work Performance* (New York: McGraw-Hill, 1999).

RECOMMENDED READING

Gale, Bradley T. *Managing Customer Value: Creating Quality and Service That Customers Can See.* New York: Free Press, 1994.

George, Michael L. *Lean Six Sigma.* New York: McGraw Hill, 2002.

Goldratt, Eliyahu M. *Theory of Constraints.* Great Barrington, MA: North River Press, 1999.

Hammer, Michael. *The Agenda.* New York: Crown Business, 2001.

Harrington, H. James. *Business Process Improvement: The Breakthrough Strategy for Total Quality, Productivity, and Competitiveness.* New York: McGraw Hill, 1991.

Harris, Michael C. *Value Leadership: Winning Competitive Advantage in the Information Age.* Milwaukee: ASQ Quality Press, 1998.

Kaplan, Robert S., and David P. Norton. *The Balanced Scorecard: Translating Strategy into Action.* Cambridge, MA: Harvard Business School Press, 1996.

Keen, Peter. *The Process Edge: Creating Value Where It Counts.* Cambridge, MA: Harvard Business School Press, 1997.

Miles, Robert H. *Leading Corporate Transformation.* San Francisco: Jossey-Bass, 1997.

Ostroff, Frank. *The Horizontal Organization.* Oxford University Press, 1999.

Pall, Gabriel A. *The Process Centered Enterprise: The Power of Commitments.* Boca Raton, FL: St. Lucie Press, 2000.

Pande, Peter S., Robert P. Neuman, and Roland R. Cavanaugh. *The Six Sigma Way.* New York: McGraw Hill, 2000.

Reichheld, Frederick F. *The Loyalty Effect: The Hidden Force Behind Growth, Profits and Lasting Value.* Boston: Bain and Company, 1996.

Rummler, Geary A., and Alan P. Brache. *Improving Performance: How to Manage the White Space on the Organization Chart.* San Francisco: Jossey-Bass Publishers, 1995.

Womack, James P., and Daniel T. Jones. *Lean Thinking.* Simon and Schuster, 1996.

Woodruff, Robert B., and Sarah Gardial. *Know Your Customer: New Approaches to Understanding Customer Value and Satisfaction.* Malden, MA: Blackwell Publishers, 1996.

Index

A

accountable, 131, 148
activity-based costing assessments, 77
activity-based costing techniques, 13
activity dictionary, 107–8
adaptability, 13–14
    process-focused organization, 42
adaptive enterprise, 13–14
alignment
    maintaining, 172
    organizational, 11–12
    process-focused organization, 42
analysis categories, 103
analysis of variance, 158
analysis paralysis, 24
appraisal costs, 34
approval, formal, 84
assessment and planning phase, 73–86
assumptions, project, 180
audit schedule and methods, 204

B

backup programs, 197–98
baseline, 65

baseline measurements, conducting, 103–4
baseline phase, 95–110
baselined process, characteristics, 65
behaviorism, 166–67
best practices, 167–68, 173
black boxes, 143
budget, 171, 180
business case, preparing, 83
business processes, 31
    identifying and grading, 77–82
business-focused process goals, 92

C

calibration programs, 197
capability problems, 156
capable process, 35–36, 156, 157
catchball, 165
change, 22–23
    adapting to, 13–14
    implementing, 172
    large-scale, 50
    process-focused organization, 42
change control system, 139
change leadership, training, 85